Fireside Feasts
& Snow Day Treats

Fireside Feasts

& Snow Day Treats

Indulgent comfort food
recipes for winter eating

RYLAND PETERS & SMALL
LONDON • NEW YORK

Senior Designer Toni Kay
Editors Julia Charles, Gillian Haslam
Production Gary Hayes, David Hearn
Art Director Leslie Harrington
Editorial Director Julia Charles
Publisher Cindy Richards

Indexer Hilary Bird

First published in the United Kingdom
in 2012. This revised edition published
in 2016 by Ryland Peters & Small
20–21 Jockey's Fields
London WC1R 4BW
and
Ryland Peters & Small, Inc.
341 E 116th St
New York NY 10029

www.rylandpeters.com

10 9 8 7 6 5 4 3 2 1

Design and commissioned
photographs © Ryland Peters & Small
2012, 2016. See page 176 for full
photography credits.

Text © 2012, 2016 Ryland Peters &
Small (and contributors as listed on
page 176).

ISBN: 978 1 84975 777 5

A catalogue record for this book
is available from the British Library.

A CIP record for this book is available
from the Library of Congress.

Printed and bound in China.

Notes

• Both British (Metric) and American
(Imperial plus US cup) measurements
are included in these recipes for your
convenience – however it is important
to work with one set of measurements
only within a recipe and not alternate
between the two.
• All spoon measurements are level,
unless otherwise stated.
• Eggs are US large/UK medium
unless otherwise specified. Uncooked
or partially cooked eggs should not
be served to the very old, frail, young
children, pregnant women or those
with compromised immune systems.
• When a recipe calls for the grated
zest of lemons or limes or uses slices
of fruit, buy unwaxed fruit and wash
well before using. If you can only find
treated fruit, scrub well in warm soapy
water before using.
• Ovens should be preheated to the
specifed temperature. Recipes in this
book were tested in a regular oven.
If using a fan-assisted oven, follow
the manufacturer's instructions for
adjusting temperatures.

contents

introduction

When the weather turns cold and the days grow short, what could be better than warming up by the fire and enjoying home-cooked food with family and friends. With flavoursome, comforting dishes for every occasion, this collection of delicious recipes will help stave off winter's chill and keep you warm the whole season through.

While the cold wind blows and the snow piles up outside, make the most of being stuck indoors and prepare some warming Snow Day Snacks. Enjoy sharing tasty treats such as Baked Goat Cheese with Herbed Ciabatta Croutons or Creamy Pancetta Tart – perfect to serve with pre-dinner drinks or as a light lunch or supper by the fire.

When it's freezing outside, what we naturally crave is warm, comforting food. In Cold Day Comforts you'll find plenty of nourishing dishes from hearty soups to sustaining risottos including Spiced Pumpkin and Coconut Soup, Corn and Pancetta Chowder and Saffron Risotto with Aged Parmesan, Sage and Serrano Ham.

What better way to spend a chilly afternoon than preparing a delicious meal to share with family and friends. Fireside Feasts is full of great ideas for winter entertaining. From roasts and pot roasts to casseroles, braises and pies, this chapter has everything you need to create a homely family feast. Try a Braised Pot Roast with Red Wine, Rosemary and Bay Leaves, Chicken Pot Pie with Tarragon and Leeks or Slow-cooked Lamb Shanks with Lentils.

Make the most of the finest seasonal ingredients the winter has to offer and prepare healthy and satisfying Winter Salads. Choose from Blue Cheese and Steak Winter Salad, a Roast Sweet Potato and Macadamia Nut Salad or Slow-cooked Lamb Salad with Beans, Pomegranate and Fresh Mint.

Baking is such a comforting pastime when holed-up indoors. Whether you enjoy a slice of cake in front of the fire or a dessert, there are plenty of sweet delights to choose from in Indulgent Treats. Try the Pecan Cheesecake Swirl Brownies, Arctic Roll with Vanilla and Chocolate or the Chocolate Chestnut Brownie Torte.

Finally, in A Cup of Cheer there are plenty of ideas for delicious drinks to enjoy while relaxing at home, as well as entertaining. Curl up on a quiet evening with a good book and enjoy a warming Hot Chocolate with Almond Cream or a Peppermint White Chocolate Dream. Get any festive gathering off to a flying start with a Black Olive Martini, a classic Mulled Wine or a Garrick Gin Punch.

snow day snacks

When the weather turns colder and the days grow short, what could be better than coming home to a warm bowl of comforting food after a long walk through the autumn leaves?

creamy pancetta and onion tart

A delicious combination of sweet, tender-cooked onions, salty pancetta and tangy crème fraîche/sour cream, all gently infused with thyme and cooked on a buttery puff pastry base. Serve simply with a rocket/arugula salad.

1 tablespoon olive oil
170 g/5½ oz. diced pancetta
3 onions, sliced
1 fat garlic clove, crushed
1 teaspoon (caster) sugar
2 sprigs of fresh thyme
375 g/12½ oz. ready made puff pastry
250 g/1 cup crème fraîche/sour cream
sea salt and freshly ground black pepper

2 solid baking sheets

Serves 4

Preheat the oven to 200°C (400°F) Gas 6 and place one of the baking sheets on the middle shelf to heat up.

Heat the olive oil in a large frying pan over medium heat, add the pancetta and cook until crisp. Remove from the pan with a slotted spoon and drain on paper towels. Add the sliced onions to the pan and cook for about 10 minutes, stirring occasionally until they start to colour. Add the garlic, sugar and leaves from the thyme sprig and cook for a further minute to caramelize the onions. Remove from the heat, stir in the pancetta and let cool slightly.

Roll out the puff pastry on a lightly floured work surface. Keep rolling until it's big enough to trim into a rectangle about 30 x 20 cm/12 x 8 inches. Using the tip of the knife, score a border 2 cm/¾ inch from the edge without cutting all the way through the pastry. Carefully lift the pastry onto the second baking sheet and slide into the preheated oven on top of the hot baking sheet. Cook for 7 minutes, then remove from the oven.

Season the crème fraîche/sour cream with salt and pepper and spread half of it over the tart base. Season the onion and pancetta mixture with salt and pepper too and spread over the crème fraîche/sour cream. Dot the remaining crème fraîche over the filling and return to the oven for a further 20 minutes, or until the pastry is golden and the filling is bubbling. Cut into slices and serve warm.

parmesan custards with anchovy toasts

These luxurious parmesan custards make a delectable appetizer or snack that will warm you up on a cold day. The salty anchovy toasts make the perfect accompaniment to the creamy texture of the custards. A perfect dish for winter entertaining at home.

300 ml/1¼ cups single/light cream
300 ml/1¼ cups whole milk
100 g/1 cup finely grated Parmesan
4 egg yolks
cayenne pepper
12 anchovy fillets
50 g/3 tablespoons unsalted butter
8 very thin slices of rustic loaf
sea salt and finely ground white pepper

8 x 80-ml/⅓-cup ramekins or ovenproof dishes, greased

Serves 8

Mix the cream, milk and all but 1 tablespoon of the Parmesan in a heatproof bowl, place it over a saucepan of boiling water, and warm it gently until the Parmesan has melted. Remove the bowl from on top of the pan and let cool completely.

Preheat the oven to 150°C (300°F) Gas 2.

Whisk the egg yolks, a pinch of salt, a pinch of white pepper, and a little cayenne pepper into the cool cream mixture, then divide between the prepared ramekins. Place the ramekins in an ovenproof dish in the oven, then pour boiling water from the kettle into the dish to reach halfway up the ramekins. Cover the whole dish with a sheet of greased parchment paper and bake in the preheated oven for 15 minutes or until the custards have just set. Remove from the oven and preheat the grill/broiler.

Mash the anchovies and butter to make a smooth paste and spread over 4 of the slices of bread. Cover with the remaining bread and toast in a sandwich maker or panini machine. Sprinkle the remaining Parmesan over the warm custards and brown gently under the hot grill/broiler. Cut the toasted anchovy sandwiches into fingers and serve alongside the custards.

leek and blue cheese quiche with hazelnut pastry

3 leeks (about 400 g/14 oz. untrimmed)

40 g butter/3 tablespoons

3 large eggs

250 ml/1 cup whipping cream

30 g/⅓ cup Parmesan, freshly grated

100 g/1 cup medium-strong blue cheese, e.g. Stilton, crumbled

sea salt and freshly ground black pepper

Hazelnut pastry

25 g/⅛ cup whole hazelnuts

75 g plain/all-purpose flour

50 g/⅓ cup wholemeal flour

75 g/⅓ cup chilled butter, cubed

3–4 tablespoons iced water

a deep 23-cm/9-inch loose-based quiche pan

baking beans

Serves 4–6

Preheat the oven to 190°C (375°F) Gas 5.

First make the pastry. Put the hazelnuts on a baking sheet and roast in the preheated oven for 10 minutes or until the skins turn dark brown. (Turn off the oven.) Leave to cool for a few minutes, then tip them onto a clean dish towel and rub off the skins. Transfer to a food processor and pulse until finely chopped, then add the flours and pulse once or twice to mix. Add the butter and pulse to combine, then add just enough of the iced water to bring the mixture together. Pat the pastry into a ball, wrap in clingfilm/plastic wrap and leave to rest in the fridge for 1 hour.

Meanwhile, trim the bases and cut the coarse outer leaves from the leeks. Thinly slice the leeks and rinse thoroughly to get rid of any dirt or grit. Heat the butter in a large frying pan and fry the leeks for 5–6 minutes until beginning to soften. Season well and set aside to cool.

Roll the pastry out to a circle to fit your quiche pan. Lower the pastry into the pan, pressing it into the edges, and lightly prick the base with a fork. Leave any overhanging pastry untrimmed. Refrigerate for 20 minutes. Preheat the oven again to 190°C (375°F) Gas 5. Line the pastry case with parchment paper, fill with baking beans and bake in the oven for about 12 minutes. Leave the oven on.

Separate 1 of the eggs, reserve the white and beat the yolk and the other 2 whole eggs together. Measure the cream in a jug/pitcher, add the beaten egg and half the Parmesan, season with pepper and beat well.

Remove the paper and beans from the pastry case and brush with the reserved egg white. Return to the oven for another 5 minutes, then remove from the oven and reduce the oven temperature to 180°C (350°F) Gas 4. Trim the overhanging edge of pastry with a knife. Scatter half the blue cheese in the pastry case, spoon over the leeks, then cover with the remaining blue cheese. Pour the egg and cream mixture over the top (only use as much as you need to fill the case). Sprinkle over the remaining Parmesan. Bake for about 35–40 minutes until the top is lightly browned. Leave to cool for 20 minutes before serving.

egg-rice pockets

200 g/1½ cups strong white bread flour

200 g/1¾ sticks unsalted butter, chilled and cubed

75 ml/5 tablespoons very cold water

Filling

100 g/½ cup short-grain rice

2 eggs, plus 1 extra, lightly beaten, for glazing

35 g/2½ tablespoons unsalted butter, melted

sea salt and freshly ground black pepper

a round cookie cutter (or an upturned cup), about 10 cm/4 inches in diameter

1–2 baking sheets, lined with non-stick parchment paper

Makes 12–16

Put the flour in a mixing bowl. Add the cubed butter and rub in using your fingertips until the mixture looks like fine breadcrumbs.

Gradually add the water to the flour mixture, stirring with a round-bladed knife until a dough forms. Wrap in clingfilm/plastic wrap and leave to rest in the refrigerator for at least 2 hours, or overnight if possible.

To make the filling, cook the rice according to the manufacturer's instructions. When the rice is ready, it should be quite sticky. Set aside to cool while you make the rest of the filling.

Put the eggs in a small saucepan of cold water and bring to a gentle boil. Simmer for 6–7 minutes, until just hard. Transfer to a bowl of cold water and immerse until the eggs are cool enough to handle. Peel and chop them finely, then mix with the melted butter and cooked rice. Season with salt and pepper to taste. Set aside.

Preheat the oven to 220°C (425°F) Gas 7.

Take the pastry out of the refrigerator and remove the clingfilm/plastic wrap. Roll the pastry out on a lightly floured surface, with a rolling pin, until about 3 mm/⅛ inch thick. It may be quite sticky, so you might need to dust more flour on the work surface.

Use the cookie cutter to cut out rounds from the pastry. Gather up the offcuts of pastry and refrigerate them briefly before rolling out and cutting out more rounds.

Drop a generous tablespoon of filling onto each pastry round. Fold in half to make a semi-circle and encase the filling. Using your fingers, pinch the edges together to seal the parcels. Arrange them on the prepared baking sheets.

Brush the beaten egg over the parcels with a pastry brush, to glaze them, then prick the top of each one once with a fork. Bake in the preheated oven for about 15 minutes, or until golden brown. Serve hot or cold.

meat pie

500 g/1 lb. 2 oz. ready made short crust pastry

Filling

100 g/½ cup short-grain rice

½ vegetable or beef stock cube

2 tablespoons rapeseed oil (or vegetable oil)

1 large onion, finely chopped

300 g/10½ oz. minced/ground beef and/or pork

1½ teaspoons ground paprika

½ teaspoon ground cayenne pepper

sea salt and freshly ground black pepper

1 egg, lightly beaten, for glazing

a baking sheet, lined with non-stick parchment paper

Serves 4–6

Chill the pastry in the refrigerator until ready to use.

To make the filling, cook the rice according to the manufacturer's instructions, but crumble the stock cube into the saucepan before starting. When the rice is ready, it should be quite sticky. Set aside to cool while you make the rest of the filling.

Heat 1 tablespoon of the oil in a frying pan and fry the onion until soft and golden. Remove the onion from the pan with a slotted spoon and set aside to cool in a mixing bowl.

Put the remaining oil in the frying pan and fry the meat, stirring often, until cooked and evenly browned. Season with the paprika, cayenne pepper and salt and pepper, to taste. Set aside to cool.

When everything has cooled down slightly, mix it all in the mixing bowl.

Preheat the oven to 200°C (400°F) Gas 6.

Take the pastry out of the refrigerator and divide into two portions. Roll one portion out on a lightly floured surface, with a rolling pin, into a rectangle about 30 x 25 cm/ 12 x 10 inches. Repeat with the other portion. Gently and loosely roll one rectangle around the rolling pin and transfer it to the prepared baking sheet for the base of the pie. Spoon the filling evenly over the surface, leaving a 2-cm/¾-inch border. Brush the border with beaten egg.

Roll the second rectangle of pastry around the rolling pin and lay it neatly over the pie filling. Seal the edges by pressing the pastry between your thumb and forefinger at regular intervals along the edge. Brush the rest of the beaten egg over the pie lid and prick it in a few places with a fork. Very lightly score diagonal lines across the top. Bake in the preheated oven for 25 minutes, or until golden brown. Serve warm or cold. It will keep in the refrigerator for 2 days.

cheddar and cider fondue

Although the classic fondue recipe is Swiss, it's perfectly possible to make it with other cheeses. This version is made from quintessentially British cheeses but Gruyère or Emmental work very well too. The key things to remember with fondue are to have your cheeses at room temperature before you start, to take the pan off the heat before adding the first batch of cheese, and to stir in a figure-of-eight rather than round and round (which makes the fondue more likely to separate). Once you've got the knack, it's simplicity itself.

about 430 g/15 oz. thinly sliced or coarsely grated cheese, e.g. 150 g/5½ oz. mature/sharp Cheddar, 150 g/5½ oz. Double Gloucester and 130 g/4½ oz. Somerset Brie (all rinds removed)

2 teaspoons cornflour/cornstarch or potato flour

175 ml/¾ cup dry but fruity (hard) cider

1 tablespoon medium-dry (hard) cider or Calvados

freshly ground white or black pepper

crusty wholemeal or granary rolls, cubed, to serve

apple wedges, to serve

a cast-iron cheese fondue set

Serves 2–3

Toss the cheese with the cornflour/cornstarch. Set aside until it has come to room temperature.

Start off the fondue on your cooker. Pour the cider into your fondue pan and heat until almost boiling. Remove from the heat and tip in about one-third of the cheese. Keep breaking up the cheese with a wooden spoon using a figure-of-eight motion.

Once the cheese has begun to melt, return it to a very low heat, stirring continuously. Gradually add the remaining cheese until you have a smooth, thick mass (this takes about 10 minutes, less with practice). If it seems too thick, add some more hot cider. Add the brandy and season with pepper (preferably white, as the grains won't show). Place over your fondue burner and serve with the cubes of bread. Use long fondue forks to dip the bread in, stirring the fondue often to prevent it solidifying. Have wedges of apple on hand to refresh you between mouthfuls of fondue.

When the snow is piling up outside and the wind is howling around the house, there is something very warming about sharing a hearty fondue with friends and family.

chicken liver parfait with fig relish and toasted brioche

This is the perfect sharing dish – just put the terrine in the middle of the table with a jar of the relish, a stack of warm toasted brioche, a pile of plates and a bundle of knives and let everyone dig in. The parfait and relish can be made 2–3 days ahead of time.

250 g/2 sticks unsalted butter

3 shallots, sliced

2 sprigs of fresh thyme

2 garlic cloves, crushed

fresh grating of nutmeg

4 tablespoons port or Madeira

1 tablespoon olive oil

500 g/1 lb. chicken livers, trimmed

sea salt and freshly ground black pepper

toasted brioche, to serve

Fig relish

125 g/4 oz. ready-to-eat dried figs, roughly chopped

50 g/⅓ cup pitted dates, roughly chopped

1 shallot, sliced

1 small eating apple, peeled, cored and finely diced

2 tablespoons light muscovado sugar

125 ml/½ cup white wine vinegar or cider vinegar

1 teaspoon grated orange zest

1 cinnamon stick

1 fresh or dried bay leaf

a pâté terrine or serving dish

Serves 4–6

Melt 2 tablespoons of the butter in a small saucepan, add the shallots and half the leaves from the thyme sprigs, and cook over low–medium heat until the shallots are soft but not coloured. Add the garlic and nutmeg and continue to cook for another minute. Add the port and cook until almost all the liquid has evaporated. Remove from the heat.

Heat the oil in a large frying pan and add half the chicken livers. Cook over medium–high heat for a couple of minutes on each side until they are just cooked through but still pink in the middle. Tip the livers and the onion mixture into a food processor. Cook the remainder of the chicken livers in the same pan, then add to the food processor. Blend until smooth. Cut 175 g/1½ sticks of the butter into small pieces and add to the mixture with the motor running. Push the mixture through a fine-mesh sieve/strainer into a bowl and season well with salt and black pepper.

Spoon the parfait into the terrine or serving dish and spread level. Gently melt the remaining butter, remove from the heat and leave for 2 or 3 minutes to allow the butter to separate from the whey. Leave the cloudy whey on the bottom and spoon the golden melted butter from the top onto the parfait to cover it. Scatter the remaining thyme leaves over the top and allow to set and cool before chilling.

To make the fig relish, tip all the ingredients into a medium saucepan. Cook over low heat for about 25 minutes, or until tender and jammy. Remove the cinnamon stick and bay leaf, season and let cool before serving with the parfait and some slices of toasted brioche.

cheese and basil soufflés

Soufflés are one of the most impressive recipes you can make for your friends – guaranteed to provoke 'oohs' and 'aaahs' from everyone around the table, especially with this unusual combination of cheese and basil. They're not as difficult as they look – you just need to keep your nerve!

200 ml/¾ cup whole milk

4–6 sprigs of fresh basil (depending how strong they are)

4 large eggs (or 5 if your whites are unusually small)

25 g/2 tablespoons butter

20 g plain/all-purpose flour

50 g/1¾ oz. mature/sharp Gruyère or Cheddar, grated

25 g/1 oz. mature Parmesan, freshly grated, plus extra to dust the soufflé dish

sea salt and freshly ground black pepper

a 15-cm/6-inch soufflé dish, 9 cm/3½ inches high, lightly greased

Serves 4 as an appetizer or 2 as a main dish

Put the milk in the pan, add the basil sprigs and bring slowly to the boil. Turn the heat right down, simmer for 1 minute, then turn off the heat and leave the basil to infuse for about 20 minutes.

Separate the eggs carefully – put the whites in a large, clean bowl and set aside 3 of the yolks to add to the sauce.

Preheat the oven to 200°C (400°F) Gas 6.

Put a large, heavy-based saucepan over medium heat, and add the butter. When that has melted, stir in the flour. Cook for a few seconds, then tip in the warm basil-infused milk through a sieve/strainer. Whisk together until smooth, then cook over low heat until thick.

Stir in the grated Gruyère and most of the Parmesan and put back over low heat until the cheese has melted. Leave to cool for 5 minutes. Stir in the 3 egg yolks one by one.

Sprinkle the inside of the buttered soufflé dish with a little Parmesan, shaking off any excess. Put the dish on a baking sheet.

Whisk the egg whites and a pinch of salt until holding their shape but not stiff. Take 2 tablespoons of the whites and fold it into the cheese base, then carefully fold in the rest of the whites without overmixing. Tip the mixture into the prepared soufflé dish, scraping the last remnants in with a rubber spatula. Sprinkle with a little more Parmesan and bake in the preheated oven for 25–30 minutes until the soufflé is well risen and browned. (Don't open the oven door or your soufflé may collapse!) Serve immediately with some new potatoes or crusty bread and a green salad.

Variation: You can make these in individual ramekins if you prefer. In this case, bake them for 20–25 minutes.

sole goujons

2 tablespoons olive oil

2 tablespoons unsalted butter

200 g/4 cups fresh, fine breadcrumbs

1 tablespoon freshly chopped flat-leaf parsley

2 teaspoons freshly chopped thyme

finely grated zest of 1 unwaxed lemon

1 teaspoon Spanish smoked paprika

450 g/1 lb. skinless sole fillets

4 tablespoons plain/all-purpose flour

2 eggs, beaten

sea salt and freshly ground black pepper

To serve

tomato ketchup

tartare sauce

oven-cooked french fries

lemon wedges

baking sheet, lined with parchment paper

Serves 4

Preheat the oven to 220°C (425°F) Gas 7.

Heat the oil and butter in a large frying pan, add the breadcrumbs and, stirring constantly, cook until golden. Tip the crumbs into a large bowl, add the chopped herbs, lemon zest and paprika and season well with salt and black pepper. Let cool.

Cut each sole fillet into strips roughly 2.5 cm/1 inch wide.

Tip the flour into one shallow dish and the beaten eggs into another. Taking one piece of fish at a time, coat it first in the flour, then the beaten eggs, then the golden breadcrumbs. Arrange the goujons on the prepared baking sheet and bake in the preheated oven for about 10 minutes, or until cooked through.

Serve immediately with tomato ketchup, tartare sauce, oven-cooked french fries and lemon wedges.

pastry cigars with halloumi

4 sheets filo/phyllo pastry, thawed if frozen

200 g/7 oz. halloumi cheese, grated

50 g/2 oz. feta cheese, crumbled

125 g/1 stick butter, melted and cooled

80 g/½ cup pitted and sliced black olives

16 small fresh mint leaves

light olive oil, for frying

a baking sheet lined with parchment paper

Makes 16

Cut each sheet of filo/phyllo pastry in half lengthwise. Stack them on top of each other, then cover with parchment paper and place a damp dish towel over the top to prevent from drying out. Combine the halloumi and feta in a bowl. Lay a sheet of filo/phyllo on a clean work surface with one of the short ends nearest to you. Brush all over with melted butter. Spoon 1 tablespoon of the cheese mixture on the end of the filo/phyllo, about 1 cm/½ inch from the edge and use your fingers to shape it into a log. Top with 2–3 slices of olive and a few mint leaves. Roll over the edge nearest to you to enclose, then fold in the sides. Brush the folded-down sides with butter, then roll up to form small cigar-shapes. Repeat to make 16 cigars, putting them on the prepared baking sheet as you go. Set a frying pan over high heat and brush with oil. Cook the pastries for 2–3 minutes, turning often, until golden and crisp. Serve warm.

leek and cheddar mini quiches

500 g/1 lb. 2 oz. ready made shortcrust pastry

2 large eggs, beaten

190 ml/¾ cup double/ heavy cream

50 ml/¼ cup milk

100 g/3½ oz. mature/sharp Cheddar, grated

1 small leek, thinly sliced

½ teaspoon salt

½ teaspoon crushed black pepper

6 x 10-cm/2½ x 4-inch loose- based tartlet pans, greased

Makes 6

Preheat the oven to 170°C (325°F) Gas 3.

Make sure you have lined the tartlet pans with the shortcrust pastry and refrigerate for 20 minutes while you make the filling.

Put the eggs, cream and milk in a bowl and mix well, then stir in the cheese, leek, salt and pepper.

Remove the tartlet shells from the fridge and fill each one with the leek mixture.

Bake in the preheated oven for 30 minutes. Remove from the oven and leave to cool before serving. Store refrigerated in an airtight container for up to 1 week.

very herby falafel with red pepper hummus

200 g/1 cup dried chickpeas

100 g/1 cup shelled broad/fava beans or butter beans

2 garlic cloves, crushed

2 tablespoons freshly chopped coriander/cilantro

2 tablespoons freshly chopped flat-leaf parsley

2 tablespoons freshly chopped mint

1 shallot, finely chopped

1 teaspoon ground cumin

1 teaspoon ground coriander

½ teaspoon ground cayenne pepper

1 teaspoon bicarbonate of soda/baking soda

freshly squeezed juice of 1 lemon

2 tablespoons sesame seeds

sea salt and freshly ground black pepper

about 1 litre/4 cups sunflower oil, for deep-frying

toasted flatbreads and pickled mild green chilli/chile peppers, to serve

Red pepper hummus

400-g/14-oz. can chickpeas

1 tablespoon tahini

4 tablespoons fruity olive oil

1 garlic clove

1 roasted red bell pepper, from a jar

freshly squeezed juice of ½ lemon

Makes 12

Soak the dried chickpeas overnight in a bowl of cold water.

The next day, drain and rinse the chickpeas. Bring a saucepan of water to the boil, add half the chickpeas and cook for about 15–20 minutes, or until tender. Add the broad/fava beans and cook for a further 2 minutes. Drain and tip into the bowl of a food processor with the remaining uncooked, soaked chickpeas.

Add the garlic, chopped herbs, shallot, spices, bicarbonate of soda/baking soda, lemon juice and 1 teaspoon salt. Season well with black pepper and whiz until almost smooth and well combined.

Tip the mixture into a bowl and roll into 12 even-sized balls, then flatten slightly to make patties. Press the sesame seeds into both sides of each falafel.

Fill a deep-fat fryer with sunflower oil or pour oil to a depth of about 4 cm/1½ inches into a deep saucepan. Heat until a cube of bread sizzles and browns in about 10 seconds. Cook the falafel in batches of 3–4 at a time in the hot fat until golden brown. Drain on paper towels.

To make the red pepper hummus, drain and rinse the canned chickpeas. Put them in the bowl of the food processor with the tahini, olive oil, garlic and red pepper and whiz until smooth. Season well with salt and black pepper and lemon juice to taste.

Serve the falafel with the red pepper hummus, toasted flatbreads, and pickled green chilli/chile peppers.

baked goat cheese with herbed ciabatta croutons and winter fruit salad

For this recipe, use goat cheese logs that have a soft white rind. In this recipe rocket/arugula has been used, as the peppery leaves contrast wonderfully with the creamy cheese, sweet pears and tangy pomegranate, but you could also use watercress or chicory/Belgian endive.

1 ciabatta loaf

4 tablespoons olive oil

2 teaspoons freshly chopped thyme

2 teaspoons freshly chopped oregano

2 x 120 g/4½-oz. goat cheese logs (with rind)

1 egg, beaten

Winter fruit salad

2 red pears

2 green pears

1 pomegranate

3 handfuls of wild rocket/arugula leaves

50 g/½ cup toasted hazelnuts, roughly chopped

2 tablespoons balsamic vinegar

5 tablespoons hazelnut oil

sea salt and freshly ground black pepper

solid baking sheet

Serves 4–6

Make the breadcrumbs and herbed ciabatta croutons first. Cut the ciabatta in half. Take one half, roughly chop and put in a food processor. Whiz until you get fine breadcrumbs. Heat half the oil in a frying pan, add the breadcrumbs and toast until golden. Remove from the pan and drain on paper towels. If the breadcrumbs are on the chunky side, whiz them again in the food processor for another 30 seconds.

Preheat the grill/broiler to medium. Slice the remaining ciabatta into long, thin slices. Mix the remaining oil with the chopped herbs and brush over one side of the bread. Toast under the hot grill/broiler, turning over once, until golden on both sides.

Preheat the oven to 180°C (350°F) Gas 4.

Trim the ends off each goat cheese log and cut each log into 3 evenly sized pieces. Dip the cheese pieces in the beaten egg, then roll in the toasted breadcrumbs to cover. Arrange on a baking sheet and cook in the preheated oven for about 7 minutes until warm and bubbling.

While the cheese is baking, make the winter fruit salad. Quarter, core and slice the pears into slim wedges. Cut the pomegranate into quarters and pick out the beautiful jewel-like seeds. Arrange the pears, pomegranate seeds and rocket/arugula on a large serving platter and scatter the chopped hazelnuts over the top.

Whisk the balsamic vinegar and hazelnut oil together and drizzle over the salad. Top with the warm cheese and the herbed ciabatta croutons and serve immediately.

carrot and chickpea pancakes with hummus and slow-roasted tomatoes

Grated carrot and courgette/zucchini are bound together here in a spicy, chickpea-flour batter. Chickpea flour (also called gram flour or besan) is available in health food or Asian food stores, but if you can't find it, use plain/all-purpose flour instead.

8–10 tomatoes

2 tablespoons olive oil

1 sprig of fresh thyme

1 tub of hummus

2 handfuls of baby salad leaves or sprouting seeds, such as alfalfa and radish

fruity extra virgin olive oil, for drizzling

Carrot & chickpea pancakes

125 g/scant 1 cup coarsely grated courgette/zucchini

125 g/1 cup coarsely grated carrot

1 garlic clove, crushed

1 tablespoon freshly chopped coriander/cilantro

1 tablespoon freshly chopped mint

½ teaspoon ground cumin

½ teaspoon ground coriander

¼ teaspoon ground cayenne pepper

125 g/1 cup chickpea flour or plain/all-purpose flour

½ teaspoon baking powder

100 g/3½ oz. feta, crumbled

100 ml/½ cup milk

1 egg, lightly beaten

sea salt and freshly ground black pepper

1 tablespoon sunflower oil

Makes 12–15 pancakes

Preheat the oven to 170°C (325°F) Gas 3.

Cut the tomatoes in half, arrange on a small baking sheet, cut-side up, and drizzle the olive oil over them. Scatter the leaves from the thyme all over the top and season with salt and black pepper. Roast on the middle shelf of the preheated oven for 30–40 minutes until soft and starting to brown at the edges. Remove from the oven and let cool to room temperature.

To make the carrot and chickpea pancakes, tip the grated courgette/zucchini, carrot, garlic, herbs, spices, flour and baking powder into a mixing bowl and stir until combined. Add the feta, milk and egg and mix into a batter. Season the mixture well with salt and pepper.

Heat half the sunflower oil in a frying pan. Add 4 separate tablespoons of the batter to the pan – one for each pancake. Cook over low–medium heat for 2 minutes, or until golden on the underside. Carefully flip the pancakes over and cook the other side until golden. Remove from the pan and keep warm while you cook the remaining batter, adding more oil to the pan as and when needed.

To serve, arrange the pancakes on plates with hummus, the slow-roasted tomatoes and baby salad leaves, drizzle olive oil over the top and serve warm.

spiced fried chicken

3 skinless chicken breasts
150 ml/⅔ cup buttermilk
100 g/¾ cup plain/
all-purpose flour
1 generous teaspoon
baking powder
1 generous teaspoon
sea salt flakes
½ teaspoon ground
cayenne pepper

½ teaspoon Spanish smoked
paprika
¼ teaspoon ground coriander
¼ teaspoon garlic powder
a pinch of ground allspice
½ teaspoon dried oregano
freshly ground black pepper
sunflower oil, for frying

Serves 4

Cut each chicken breast into 5 or 6 strips. Place in a ceramic
dish and coat with the buttermilk. Cover with clingfilm/plastic
wrap and chill for at least 2 hours.

Remove the chicken from the buttermilk. Combine the flour,
baking powder, salt flakes, spices, oregano and some black
pepper in a bowl. Toss the chicken pieces in the seasoned
flour and set aside for 10 minutes.

Pour 3–4 tablespoons sunflower oil in a frying pan. Set over
medium heat and add one-third of the chicken pieces. Cook
until golden and crispy. Drain on paper towels and repeat
with the remaining 2 batches of chicken. Serve immediately.

sticky spare ribs with honey and soy glaze

1 kg/2 lbs. short or loin pork ribs/country-style pork spare ribs

4 garlic cloves, crushed

2 tablespoons grated fresh ginger

4 tablespoons clear honey

2 tablespoons soy sauce

2 tablespoons hoisin sauce

2 tablespoons sweet chilli/chili sauce

2 tablespoons tamarind paste

¼ teaspoon Chinese five-spice powder

large roasting dish

Serves 4–6

Place the ribs in a saucepan of water, bring to the boil and simmer for 5–10 minutes, then drain.

Mix the remaining ingredients together in a large bowl, add the ribs and stir thoroughly to coat. Let cool and allow to marinate for about 30 minutes.

Preheat the oven to 190°C (375°F) Gas 5.

Tip the ribs and marinade into a large roasting dish, cover with foil and cook on the middle shelf of the preheated oven for about 20 minutes. Remove the foil, turn the ribs over, basting them with the marinade, and cook for another 20 minutes until sticky and browned all over. Allow to rest for a couple of minutes before serving.

warm spice-rubbed potatoes with rosemary mayonnaise

For the mayonnaise:

3 egg yolks

3 tablespoons fresh rosemary needles

1 teaspoon Dijon mustard

3 tablespoons cider vinegar

500 ml/2 cups grapeseed oil

For the potatoes:

750 g/1½ lbs. pink-skinned new potatoes, halved lengthwise

1 teaspoon cayenne pepper

1 teaspoon caraway seeds

1 teaspoon coriander seeds

a small piece of cinnamon stick

1 garlic clove, crushed

1 teaspoon sea salt

2 tablespoons olive oil

cocktail sticks/toothpicks or small forks

Serves 12

To make the mayonnaise, put all the ingredients, except the grapeseed oil, in a food processor and blend. With the motor running, slowly add the oil in droplets until the mayonnaise starts to thicken. Continue with an even trickle until you have incorporated all the oil. Spoon into a bowl and chill.

For the potatoes, cook the potatoes in a large pan of boiling water for about 12–15 minutes, until almost cooked. Drain and pat dry.

Preheat the oven to 400°F (200°C) Gas 6.

Gently warm the spices in a small pan for about 2 minutes until their scent starts to pervade the kitchen. Put the warmed spices, garlic, and salt in the clean food processor and blend to make a rough spice mix.

Put the potatoes in a bowl with the olive oil and toss together. Using clean hands, rub the spice mixture onto the potatoes and bake them on a baking sheet in the preheated oven for about 20 minutes until golden. Serve with the rosemary mayonnaise, for dipping.

spicy bean dip

Shiny, black kidney-shaped black beans are popular in Latin American cooking. They are left whole in this recipe but you could roughly mash after cooking to make them more gooey.

440 g/1 lb. dried black beans

2 tablespoons olive oil

1 red onion, chopped

4 garlic cloves, chopped

1 red bell pepper, deseeded and diced

1 tablespoon ground cumin

2 teaspoons dried Greek oregano

2 teaspoons chilli/chili powder

2 x 400-g/14-oz. cans chopped tomatoes

a handful of fresh coriander/cilantro leaves, chopped

plain yogurt, to serve

warmed corn chips, to serve

Serves 6–8

Put the dried beans in a saucepan with 2 litres/8 cups cold water. Bring to the boil, then reduce the heat to low and simmer the beans, uncovered, for about 1½ hours, until just tender and not falling apart. Drain well and set aside.

Heat the oil in a large, heavy-based saucepan set over medium heat. When the oil is hot, add the onion, garlic and red pepper and cook for 8–10 minutes, until softened. Stir in the cumin, oregano and chilli/chili powder and fry for 1 minute, until the spices are aromatic.

Increase the heat to high. Add the tomatoes, beans and 250 ml/1 cup cold water and bring to the boil. Reduce the heat to low, partially cover the pan and cook for 1½–2 hours, adding a little more water from time to time if the mixture is drying or catching on the bottom of the pan. Transfer to a serving bowl and serve with the yogurt and coriander/cilantro on top and corn chips for dipping.

spicy pork satay with roast salted peanut sauce

These spicy pork skewers dipped in peanut sauce are heaven on a stick. They are great for weekend get-togethers with family and friends, when you want to make delicious, easy food with minimum kitchen time.

450 g/1 lb. pork tenderloin

coriander/cilantro leaves and lime wedges, to garnish

Spicy marinade

2 tablespoons rice wine vinegar

2 green chillies/chiles, chopped

1 tablespoon soy sauce

1 large garlic clove, finely chopped

1 tablespoon toasted sesame oil

2 tablespoons fish sauce

2 tablespoons peanut oil

2 tablespoons chopped coriander/cilantro leaves

1 tablespoon grated fresh ginger

Roast salted peanut sauce

1 tablespoon peanut oil

1 garlic clove, finely chopped

2 red Thai chillies/chiles, finely chopped

4 kaffir lime leaves

1 stalk lemongrass, cut into 4

1 teaspoon garam masala or curry powder

2 tablespoons dark brown soft sugar

225 g/1 cup peanut butter

250 ml/1 cup coconut milk

30 g/½ cup unsweetened coconut flakes

finely grated zest and freshly squeezed juice of 1 lime

2 tablespoons fish sauce

18–20 wooden skewers, soaked in cold water for 30 minutes

a ridged stovetop griddle/grill pan

Makes 18–20 skewers

Slice the pork into ½-cm/¼-inch thick pieces and put in a bowl. Mix together all the Spicy Marinade ingredients and pour over the pork. Cover and put in the refrigerator for 30 minutes.

To make the Roast Salted Peanut Sauce, heat the peanut oil in a saucepan over medium heat. Sauté the garlic, chillies/chiles, kaffir lime leaves, lemongrass and garam masala for 2 minutes. Add the sugar and stir. Now add the peanut butter, coconut milk and coconut flakes, along with the lime zest and juice. Cook for 15 minutes. Take off the heat and stir in the fish sauce. Pour the mixture into a bowl and set aside.

Remove the pork from the refrigerator and thread onto the soaked wooden skewers.

Heat the griddle/grill pan over high heat until nearly smoking. Grill the pork skewers for 3–4 minutes each side until brown and caramelized.

Top the pork skewers with coriander/cilantro leaves and serve with lime wedges and the Roast Salted Peanut Sauce for dipping.

olive suppli

Traditional suppli have mozzarella inside but these have a cured black olive in the centre which makes for a delicious surprise. It's a perfect party dish for the winter, and also a marvellous way to use up any leftover risotto.

17 cured black olives, pitted

40 g/⅓ cup plain/all-purpose flour

2 eggs, beaten

140 g/3 cups fresh breadcrumbs

vegetable oil, for frying

saffron salt, to sprinkle

Risotto

20 g/1 cup dried porcini mushrooms

250 ml/1 cup white wine

500 ml/2 cups chicken stock

2 tablespoons olive oil

1 garlic clove, finely chopped

2 tablespoons thyme leaves

1 tablespoon chopped fresh rosemary

200 g/1 cup arborio rice

60 g/2¼ oz. Parmesan, grated

sea salt and cracked black pepper

Makes 17

For the risotto, soak the mushrooms in the wine for 30 minutes. Drain, reserving the liquid, and chop roughly. Pour the reserved liquid into a small pan with the chicken stock. Bring to the boil and reduce to a simmer.

Put the olive oil, garlic, thyme, rosemary and mushrooms in a medium pan and cook over medium-high heat for a few seconds, coating with the olive oil. Add the rice and stir for 2–3 minutes until well coated and translucent. Start adding the stock a ladleful at a time, stirring continuously until the liquid has been absorbed. Continue until you have used all the liquid, about 20 minutes. Stir in the cheese and season with salt and pepper. Pour onto a large plate and spread out to cool.

To make the suppli, take tablespoons of cooled risotto and form 17 balls. With your forefinger make a dent in each risotto ball and place an olive in the centre. Roll the risotto ball in your hand to reshape and cover the olive.

Dust the suppli balls with flour, dip into the beaten egg, and then toss in the breadcrumbs until well coated. At this stage they can be left to rest in the refrigerator for up to 6 hours until you are ready to cook.

Heat the oil in a heavy-based pan until the oil reaches 180°C (350°F). Alternatively, test the oil by dropping in a cube of bread. It should turn golden brown in 20 seconds.

Fry the suppli in batches until crispy and golden brown, about 2 minutes. Drain on paper towels. Sprinkle generously with saffron salt and serve immediately.

salt cod, potato and butter bean fritters

Salt cod is a very full-flavoured ingredient and one of the most popular foods of Spain and Portugal. Potatoes make the perfect partner to the cod in these light and crispy fritters and are the traditional ingredient but the addition of butter beans makes them smoother and creamier. Serve with plenty of lemon wedges for squeezing and a little aioli, if liked.

400 g/14 oz. salt cod
200 g/7 oz. floury potatoes, quartered
50 g/⅔ cup canned butter beans, drained and rinsed
2 tablespoons milk
2 tablespoons olive oil
2 garlic cloves, crushed
30 g/⅓ cup plain/all-purpose flour
¼ teaspoon baking powder
2 eggs, separated
2 spring onions/scallions, finely chopped
a small handful of fresh flat leaf parsley leaves, finely chopped
light olive oil, for frying
lemon wedges, to serve

Makes about 36

Soak the salt cod in cold water for 24 hours, changing the water every 6 hours.

Cook the potatoes in boiling water for 15 minutes, until tender. Add the beans and cook for 5 minutes. Drain well and put into a bowl. Mash with the milk and oil until chunky and well combined.

Drain the cod and cut into large chunks. Put into a saucepan and add sufficient water to fully submerge the cod. Bring to the boil and cook for 10–15 minutes, until the water surface is frothy and the fish is tender. Drain and let cool for a few minutes. When cool enough to handle, pick out any bones and flake the flesh with a fork.

Add the cod to the potatoes with the garlic, flour, baking powder, egg yolks, spring onions/scallions and parsley. Whisk the egg whites until peaking then fold into the potato mixture until combined.

Fill a heavy-based saucepan one-third full with oil and heat over medium-high heat. The oil is ready when the surface is shimmering and a pinch of the fritter mixture sizzles on contact. Drop heaped tablespoons of the fritter mixture into the hot oil, without overcrowding the pan, and cook for about 2 minutes, until golden and puffed. Transfer to a plate lined with paper towels.

meat balls with spiced tomato sauce

You can prepare these flavourful meatballs and their spiced tomato sauce ahead and reheat in a covered casserole dish either in a moderate oven or on the stovetop. They actually taste better if you make them 24 hours in advance.

3 tablespoons olive oil
2 onions, finely chopped
3 fat garlic cloves, crushed
1 teaspoon dried oregano
½ teaspoon dried chilli/hot pepper flakes
½ teaspoon ground cumin
200 ml/¾ cup red wine
400 g/14 oz. can chopped tomatoes
1 strip of orange peel
1 teaspoon granulated sugar
sea salt and freshly ground black pepper

Meat Balls
200 g/6½ oz. good-quality pork sausages
350 g/12 oz. lean minced/ground beef
1 teaspoon smoked paprika
½ teaspoon ground cumin
2 generous tablespoons freshly chopped flat-leaf parsley, plus extra to garnish
1 small egg, beaten
3 tablespoons fresh white breadcrumbs
1 tablespoon milk

Serves 4–6

Heat 2 tablespoons of the oil in a frying pan and fry the onions until soft but not coloured. Add the garlic and oregano and continue to cook for 1 minute. Scoop half the onions into a bowl and let cool.

Add the dried chilli/hot pepper flakes and cumin to the pan and cook for 30 seconds. Add the red wine, chopped tomatoes and orange peel and cook for about 30 minutes, or until the sauce has thickened slightly. Season well with salt, pepper and the sugar. Remove from the heat and set aside while you prepare the meat balls.

To make the meat balls, remove the skin from the sausages and add the meat to the cooled, cooked onions along with the beef, paprika, ground cumin, parsley, egg, breadcrumbs and milk. Using your hands, mix until combined, season well with salt and pepper, then roll into 20 walnut-sized balls.

Heat the remaining oil in a large frying pan and brown the meat balls in batches, adding more oil if necessary.

Add the meat balls to the spiced tomato sauce and cook gently over low heat for a further 30 minutes. Top with chopped parsley before serving.

spicy potatoes

2 large potatoes

2 orange-fleshed sweet potatoes

4 tablespoons olive oil

1 onion, chopped

2 garlic cloves, sliced

1 teaspoon coriander seeds

1 teaspoon cumin seeds

1 teaspoon smoked paprika

big pinch of crushed dried chillies/hot pepper flakes

150 g/5 oz. cherry tomatoes

sea salt and freshly ground black pepper

freshly chopped flat-leaf parsley, to garnish

Serves 4

Preheat the oven to 225°C (425°F) Gas 7.

Peel and cut the potatoes into large, bite-size chunks, tip into a saucepan of salted water and bring to the boil. Cook over medium heat for about 5–7 minutes. Drain and leave the potatoes to dry in the colander.

Peel and cut the sweet potato into chunks the same size as the other potatoes and tip into a roasting dish. Add the blanched potatoes, drizzle half the olive oil over them and roast in the preheated oven for about 30 minutes, or until lightly golden and tender.

Meanwhile, heat the remaining olive oil in a frying pan. Add the onion and cook for 2–3 minutes until tender but not coloured. Add the garlic and spices and cook for another 2 minutes until golden and fragrant. Add the cherry tomatoes to the pan and continue to cook until they start to soften.

Tip the contents of the pan into the roasting dish with the potatoes, season with salt and black pepper, stir to combine and return to the oven for another 5 minutes.

Serve warm, garnished with the chopped parsley.

popcorn with spiced salt

This spicy popcorn is the perfect snack for a cosy movie night at home. It is best enjoyed with a glass of cold beer to calm its fiery kick.

4 tablespoons coarse salt flakes
2 tablespoons chipotle chilli/chili powder, or to taste
2 bags unsalted microwave popcorn

Serves 4

In a small bowl, mix together the salt and chilli/chili powder. Cook the popcorn according to the package instructions. When it has popped, put in a large bowl, sprinkle with the spicy salt, and toss to mix.

golden potato crisps with truffle salt

500 g/1 lb. 2 oz. Mayan Gold potatoes or similar (about 6 small), skin on

vegetable oil, for deep-frying

truffle salt, to sprinkle

an electric deep-fat fryer

Serves 4–6

Wash and dry the potatoes, slice thinly and set aside.

Heat the oil in the deep-fat fryer or a heavy-based pan until it reaches 180°C (350°F). To test if the oil is hot enough, drop a cube of bread in the oil and it should turn golden brown in about 20 seconds.

Fry the potato slices in batches and drain on paper towels.

Put the drained potato crisps in a bowl, sprinkle with the truffle salt, toss, and serve.

goat cheese and anchovy palmiers

500 g/1 lb. 2 oz. ready made puff pastry
100 g/½ cup minus 1 tablespoon goat cheese spread or crumbled soft goat cheese
50 g/2⅔ tablespoons canned anchovies, chopped
2 tablespoons freshly chopped thyme

Makes 32

Preheat the oven to 200°C (400°F) Gas 6.

Cut the pastry in half. Take one half and put it on a lightly floured surface. Roll out into a rectangle approximately 20 x 30 cm/8 x 12 inches. Spread with half the goat cheese and scatter with half the anchovies and thyme. Repeat this process with the other piece of pastry. Roll the shorter sides tightly into the centre and squash together. Cut into slices about 2 cm/¾ inch thick and place on 2 baking sheets. Flatten each one well with the palm of your hand. Bake in the preheated oven for 20–25 minutes until golden. Let cool completely before serving.

oat biscuits for cheese

210 g/1⅔ cups plain/all-purpose flour
50 g/½ cup buckwheat flour
½ teaspoon bicarbonate of soda/baking soda
1½ teaspoons fine sea salt
¼ teaspoon ground pepper

250 g/2 sticks plus 1 tablespoon softened butter,
3 egg whites
160 g/½ rolled oats

cookie cutters in different sizes
baking sheets lined with parchment paper

Makes about 45

Sift the flours, bicarbonate of soda/baking soda, salt and pepper into a bowl. Put the butter and egg whites in a food processor and whizz until smooth. Add half the flour mixture and pulse to amalgamate, then the remaining flour and finally the oats. . Form the dough into a flat disc, wrap in clingfilm/plastic wrap and leave to rest in the fridge for at least 1 hour.

Preheat the oven to 190°C (375°F) Gas 5.

Divide the dough into 4. Roll each quarter out thinly and stamp out rounds with the cutters. Transfer carefully to the prepared baking sheets and bake in the preheated oven for 12–15 minutes until lightly coloured and crisp.

tapenade and parmesan cheese straws

1 egg, beaten
2 tablespoons whole milk
375 g/13 oz. ready made puff pastry
75 g/1 cup finely grated Parmesan
3 tablespoons black olive tapenade

Makes 15

Preheat the oven to 200°C (400°F) Gas 6.

Mix the egg with the milk. Cut the pastry in half. Take one half and put it on a lightly floured surface. Roll out into a 30-cm/12-inch square. Repeat with the other half. Brush one sheet with egg wash. Scatter with two-thirds of the Parmesan. Spread the other sheet with tapenade and place on top of the first sheet, spread-side down. Press gently and glaze again with the remaining egg wash. Cut into 1-cm/½-inch strips, twist several times and transfer to 2 baking sheets. Scatter with the rest of the cheese and bake in the preheated oven for 15–18 minutes until golden.

cheddar and cracked pepper straws

150 g/1 cup plus
2 tablespoons plain/
all-purpose flour

¼ teaspoon English mustard powder

a pinch of sea salt

100 g/7 tablespoons chilled unsalted butter, cubed

150 g/5½ oz. mature/sharp Cheddar, coarsely grated

2 tablespoons coarsely ground black pepper

1 egg yolk

1–2 baking sheets, greased

Serves 6–8

Sift the flour, mustard powder and salt into a bowl. Cut in the butter and rub together with your fingertips as if you were making pastry. Add the Cheddar and pepper and rub in thoroughly. Beat the egg yolk with 2 tablespoons water and add just enough of this mixture to the flour to enable you to pull it together into a dough. Shape into a flat disc, wrap in clingfilm/plastic wrap and refrigerate for 30 minutes. Remove from the refrigerator and leave to return to room temperature.

Preheat the oven to 190°C (375°F) Gas 5.

Roll out the dough thinly, then cut into strips about 30 cm/12 inches long. Lay the strips carefully on the prepared baking sheets and bake in the preheated oven for 12–15 minutes until golden brown. Leave on the sheets for 10 minutes, then carefully transfer to a wire rack to finish cooling. Eat fresh, ideally, but they will keep well for a couple of days in an airtight container.

cold day
comforts

Autumn and winter yields such delicious seasonal produce. Make the most of leeks, carrots, pumpkins and squash by preparing hearty soups, creamy risottos and other warming dishes.

French onion soup

50 g/3½ tablespoons butter
1 kg/2 lbs. 4 oz. onions, sliced
2 garlic cloves, crushed
1 tablespoon granulated sugar
2 tablespoons Cognac or brandy
300 ml/1¼ cups dry (hard) cider
1.2 litres/scant 5 cups beef stock
1 bouquet garni (1 sprig each of parsley, thyme and bay)
sea salt and freshly ground black pepper

For the garlic toasts

4 tablespoons extra virgin olive oil
1 garlic clove, crushed
1 small baguette or ½ large baguette, sliced
200 g/7 oz. Gruyère cheese, grated

Serves 4

Preheat the oven to 180°C (350°F) Gas 4.

To make the garlic toasts, mix the olive oil and garlic together and season well. Arrange the baguette slices on a baking sheet and brush with the garlic oil. Bake in the preheated oven for 25 minutes until crisp.

Melt the butter in a large saucepan or casserole dish over medium heat. Add the onions and garlic and stir until starting to soften. Turn the heat to low, cover and cook gently for 25–30 minutes until soft.

Take the lid off and add the sugar. Cook for a further 20 minutes, stirring until golden brown and extremely floppy-looking. This is the secret to a successful onion soup. Pour in the Cognac and cider and leave to bubble up for 1 minute. Add the stock and bouquet garni and stir to blend. Simmer for 45 minutes, then season to taste. Remove the bouquet garni.

Preheat the grill/broiler.

Divide the soup between 4 ovenproof bowls and place them on a baking sheet. Float 2–3 garlic toasts on top of each bowl and scatter the Gruyère cheese over the toasts. Grill/broil until the cheese is bubbling and golden. Remove the baking sheet and lift off the hot bowls with an oven glove/oven mitt, warning everyone that they are hot.

minestrone with parmesan rind

You can save any Parmesan rinds you may have and store them in an airtight container in the refrigerator. Use them for soups like this to add a depth of flavour.

4 tablespoons extra virgin olive oil, plus extra to serve

2 carrots, chopped

1 red onion, chopped

4 celery stalks, diced and leaves reserved

6 garlic cloves, sliced

2 tablespoons freshly chopped flat-leaf parsley

2 teaspoons tomato purée/paste

400 g/14 oz. canned peeled plum tomatoes, chopped

1 litre/4 cups chicken or vegetable stock

400-g/14-oz. can borlotti beans, drained and rinsed

Parmesan rind (optional)

150 g/5½ oz. cavolo nero or spring greens, shredded

100 g/3½ oz. spaghetti, broken up

grated Parmesan, to serve

sea salt and freshly ground black pepper

Serves 4–6

Heat the olive oil in a large, heavy-based saucepan, then add the carrots, onion, celery and garlic. Cover and sweat very slowly over low heat, stirring occasionally, until thoroughly softened.

Add the parsley, tomato purée/paste and canned tomatoes and cook for 5 minutes. Pour in the stock and borlotti beans and bring to the boil. If using a Parmesan rind, add this now. Once boiling, add the cavolo nero and simmer for 20 minutes.

Add the spaghetti and cook for 2–3 minutes less than the manufacturer's instructions suggest (by the time you have ladled it into bowls it will be perfectly cooked). Taste and adjust the seasoning.

Divide the soup between 4–6 bowls and drizzle with extra olive oil. Serve with a bowl of grated Parmesan to sprinkle over the top.

cauliflower and stilton soup

Cauliflower has a gentle spiciness and creaminess which make for wonderful soups. The Stilton can be replaced with Gorgonzola or Roquefort if you prefer. The Pear, Date and Pine Nut Relish is a lovely touch to add here, but it is best made in advance of the soup.

1 cauliflower

1 litre/4 cups chicken or vegetable stock

25 g/2 tablespoons butter

1 onion, chopped

2 celery stalks, chopped

1 leek, chopped

4 fresh thyme sprigs, leaves only

4 dried bay leaves

150 g/5½ oz. Stilton

75 ml/scant ⅓ cup crème fraîche/sour cream

sea salt and freshly ground black pepper

Pear, Date and Pine Nut Relish (page 48), to serve

Serves 4

Pull the outer leaves off the cauliflower, cut off the stem and chop it up. Put these bits into a saucepan with the stock. Bring to the boil and simmer until ready to use. Chop the cauliflower florets into 5-cm/2-inch pieces.

Melt the butter in another saucepan and cook the onion, celery and leek, covered, over low heat for 10–15 minutes until soft but not coloured.

Add the cauliflower florets, thyme, bay leaves and seasoning. Strain the stock into the pan, discarding the bits and simmer for a further 20–25 minutes until the cauliflower is very soft.

Transfer the contents of the pan, in batches, to a blender and liquidize until smooth, returning each batch back to the pan in which you cooked the stock. Place over low heat and add the Stilton and crème fraîche/sour cream. Heat, stirring, until melted. Season to taste.

Divide the soup between warmed mugs and spoon the Pear, Date and Pine Nut Relish over the top. Serve hot.

pea and smoked ham soup with mint

3 tablespoons olive oil, plus extra to serve

6 spring onions/scallions, chopped

2 garlic cloves, sliced

200 g/7 oz. thick slices of smoked ham, finely chopped

10 g/½ cup fresh mint leaves or 1 teaspoon dried mint

500 g/1 lb. 4 oz. peas (defrosted or fresh)

1 litre/4 cups hot chicken or vegetable stock

sea salt and freshly ground black pepper

Serves 4

Heat the olive oil in a large saucepan over low heat and add the spring onions/scallions. Cook for 2–3 minutes, then add the garlic, ham and half the mint and cook for a further 2 minutes, stirring frequently. Stir in the peas and pour in the hot stock. Simmer for 2–3 minutes until the peas are tender.

Transfer a third of the soup to a blender and liquidize until completely smooth. Pour back into the soup and mix until amalgamated. Season with just a little salt (the ham will be quite salty already) and pepper. Add the remaining mint.

Divide the soup between 4 bowls and serve with a drizzle of olive oil and a fresh grinding of black pepper.

split pea and sausage soup

2 tablespoons olive oil

1 onion, chopped

1 leek, chopped

2 celery stalks, chopped

a pinch of grated nutmeg

300 g/1½ cups yellow split peas

1.5 litres/6 cups chicken stock

2 dried bay leaves

250 g/9 oz. sausages

sea salt and freshly ground black pepper

Serves 6

Heat the olive oil in a large saucepan and cook the onion, leek and celery gently over low heat for 8–10 minutes. Stir in the nutmeg. Add the split peas and mix to combine with the vegetables. Add the stock and bay leaves, cover and simmer for 45 minutes or until the peas are tender and beginning to get mushy when pressed with the back of a spoon.

Meanwhile, grill/broil the sausages under medium heat until cooked, then roughly chop. Add to the soup and cook for a further 10 minutes. Season to taste with salt and pepper. Divide the soup between 6 bowls and serve immediately

corn and pancetta chowder

A chowder normally contains fish but corn replaced the fish in this recipe. The principle is still the same however – a creamy stock thickened with potatoes and spiked with the rich flavour of smoky bacon.

40 g/3 tablespoons butter

150 g/5½ oz. pancetta, cubed

1 onion, sliced

2 carrots, finely chopped

300 g/10½ oz. new potatoes (unpeeled),

thinly sliced

2 tablespoons plain/all-purpose flour

600 ml/2⅓ cups whole milk

400 ml/1⅔ cup chicken or vegetable stock

3 dried bay leaves

300 g/1½ cups (sweet) corn kernals (thawed if frozen)

3 tablespoons double/heavy cream

sea salt and freshly ground black pepper

Serves 4

Heat the butter in a large saucepan over medium heat and fry the pancetta until crisp. Add the onion, carrots and potatoes, cover and cook gently for 15–20 minutes until soft. Stir occasionally.

Sprinkle the flour into the pan and cook for 1 minute, stirring it into the vegetables. Pour in the milk gradually, blending it with the flour, then add the stock and bay leaves; bring to a gentle simmer. Add the (sweet) corn and cook for 5 minutes.

Remove from the heat, stir in the cream and season with salt. Divide the soup between 4 bowls and serve immediately with a fresh grinding of black pepper.

lentil, spinach and cumin soup

3 tablespoons extra virgin olive oil

2 onions, sliced

4 garlic cloves, sliced

1 teaspoon ground coriander

1 teaspoon cumin seeds

150 g/1½ cups brown or green lentils

1.2 litres/scant 5 cups vegetable stock

200 g/scant 3 cups spinach

freshly squeezed juice of 1 lemon

sea salt and freshly ground black pepper

To serve

4 tablespoons plain yogurt

25 g/¼ cup pine nuts, toasted

Serves 4

Heat the olive oil in a large, heavy-based saucepan and add the onions. Cook, covered, for 8–10 minutes until softened. Remove half the onion and set aside.

Continue to cook the onion left in the pan for a further 10 minutes until deep brown, sweet and caramelized. Take out and set aside for the garnish.

Return the softened onion to the pan and add the garlic, coriander, cumin seeds and lentils and stir for 1–2 minutes until well coated in oil. Add the stock, bring to the boil, then lower the heat and simmer gently for 30 minutes until the lentils are soft.

Add the spinach and stir until wilted. Transfer half the soup to a blender and liquidize until you have a purée. Stir back into the soup. Season with lemon juice, salt and pepper.

Divide the soup between 4 bowls, add a spoonful of plain yogurt and scatter the pine nuts and fried onions over the top and serve immediately.

spiced pumpkin and coconut soup

1 kg/2 lbs. 4 oz. pumpkin or butternut squash, peeled and cut into 3-cm/2-inch cubes

1 onion, cut into wedges

½ teaspoon dried chilli/hot pepper flakes

1 teaspoon ground coriander

1 teaspoon ground ginger

4 tablespoons extra virgin olive oil

3 whole garlic cloves, peeled

800 ml/3⅓ cups chicken stock

100 ml/⅓ cup coconut milk

2 tablespoons fish sauce

freshly squeezed juice of 1 lime

freshly ground black pepper

To serve

double/heavy cream

chopped red chillies/chiles (optional)

Serves 4–6

Preheat the oven to 200°C (400°F) Gas 6.

Put the pumpkin, onion, dried chilli/hot pepper flakes, coriander, ginger and olive oil in a large roasting pan and toss well. Cover with kitchen foil and roast in the preheated oven for 40 minutes, stirring halfway through, until almost soft.

Remove the foil and discard, add the garlic cloves and return to the oven for a further 20 minutes or until the garlic is tender.

When the pumpkin is soft, transfer the contents of the roasting pan to a blender (or use a handheld blender) and liquidize with half the stock until smooth. Return to the pan and add the remaining stock and the coconut milk. Bring to the boil and simmer for about 10 minutes to allow the flavours to mingle. Stir in the fish sauce and lime juice and taste for seasoning – if it needs more salt, add a dash more fish sauce.

Divide the soup between 4–6 bowls, drizzle with cream and finish with a fresh grinding of black pepper or some chopped red chillies/chiles.

apple, parsnip and thyme soup

1 small onion, chopped

2 tablespoons olive oil

1 teaspoon mild curry powder

a few sprigs of fresh thyme

450 g/1 lb. parsnips, chopped

1 large tart cooking apple, such as Bramley's, peeled, cored and roughly chopped

1.25 litres/5 cups chicken or vegetable stock

1 tablespoon unsalted butter

3 heaped tablespoons crème fraîche/sour cream, plus extra to serve

croûtons, to serve (optional)

sea salt and freshly ground black pepper

Serves 4

Put the onion, oil, curry powder and a good pinch of salt in a large saucepan. Cook gently over low heat until the onions are soft. Add the thyme, parsnips and apple and stir well. Cook for about 5 minutes, adding a little more oil if it needs it and stirring often. Add the stock and season to taste.

Simmer gently, uncovered, for about 15–20 minutes until the parsnips are soft. Purée the soup with a handheld blender, or transfer to a food processor, returning to the saucepan once blended. Taste and adjust the seasoning.

Stir in the butter and the crème fraîche/sour cream and mix well. Ladle the soup into serving bowls and top with croûtons (if using) and an extra spoonful of crème fraîche/sour cream. Serve immediately.

beef, tamarind and sweet potato soup

3 garlic cloves, peeled

2 shallots, chopped

2 green chillies/chiles, deseeded and chopped

450 g/1 lb. beef brisket or braising steak

2 tablespoons groundnut oil

1.5 litres/6 cups hot beef stock

4 tablespoons tamarind paste

4 kaffir lime leaves

2 sweet potatoes, peeled and cut into 2-cm/¾-inch chunks

150 g/5½ oz. egg noodles

1 tablespoon clear honey

sea salt

To serve

a handful of fresh mint and coriander/cilantro

2 shallots, sliced

1 fresh red chilli/chile sliced

Serves 4

Pound together the garlic, shallots and chillies/chiles with a pestle and mortar or in a spice grinder.

Blanch the beef in a pan of boiling water for 1 minute, then drain. Rinse the beef to get rid of any impurities, then cut into thin slices.

Heat the groundnut oil in a heavy-based casserole dish, then add the beef and brown evenly. Add the spice paste and toss for 1–2 minutes until fragrant, but don't allow it to burn. Add the beef stock, tamarind paste and lime leaves and simmer for 2 hours until the beef is really tender.

Add the sweet potatoes and simmer for 30 minutes until tender. Season with honey and salt to taste.

Pile up the mint, coriander/cilantro, shallots and chilli/chile on a plate and keep in the fridge until you're ready to serve. Divide the soup between 4 bowls. Serve with the plate of condiments.

Vietnamese beef pho

1 tablespoon sunflower oil

1 star anise

2 lemongrass stalks, sliced

1 cinnamon stick

1 tablespoon coriander seeds

1 tablespoon peppercorns

2.5 cm/1 inch fresh ginger, sliced

4 garlic cloves, bruised

1.5 litres/6 cups beef stock

3 fresh coriander/cilantro sprigs, roots included

150 g/5½ oz. rice noodles

4 tablespoons freshly squeezed lime juice

2 tablespoons fish sauce

200 g/7 oz. sirloin steak, sliced

100 g/1 cup beansprouts

3 shallots, thinly sliced

To serve

10 g/⅓ cup fresh Thai basil leaves

5 g/¼ cup fresh mint leaves

1 fresh red chilli/chile, sliced

lime wedges

Serves 4

Heat the sunflower oil in a large saucepan over low heat, then add the anise, lemongrass, cinnamon, coriander seeds, peppercorns, ginger and garlic. Cook gently for 1–2 minutes to release their aromas. Pour in the stock and bring to the boil.

Add the coriander/cilantro sprigs and simmer for 30 minutes. Take off the heat and leave to infuse while you prepare the other ingredients.

Get ready a plate of condiments. Pile up the Thai basil, mint, chilli/chile and lime wedges on a plate and keep in the fridge until you're ready.

When you're ready to eat, cook the rice noodles in a large pan of boiling water according to the manufacturer's instructions. Drain and refresh under cold running water. Divide between 4 bowls.

Strain the stock back into the pan and add lime juice and fish sauce to taste. Add the beef and cook for 1 minute, or until it is just cooked through. Ladle the beef and stock onto the noodles and scatter the beansprouts and shallots over the top. Serve with the plate of condiments.

seafood tom yam

1 litre/4 cups chicken stock

1 lemongrass stalk, halved lengthways and bruised

2.5 cm/1 inch fresh ginger, peeled and thinly sliced

3 kaffir lime leaves

a small handful of fresh coriander/cilantro, stalks finely chopped and leaves left whole

2 shallots, sliced

3 fresh red chillies/chiles, sliced

150 g/1½ cups halved button mushrooms

200 g/7 oz. raw king prawns/ shrimp, deveined and shelled but tails left intact

80 ml/scant ⅓ cup freshly squeezed lime juice

2 tablespoons sugar

4 tablespoons fish sauce

Serves 4–6

Put the stock in a large saucepan with the lemongrass, ginger, lime leaves, chopped coriander/cilantro stalks, shallots, chillies/chiles and mushrooms. Bring to the boil, turn down the heat and simmer for 10 minutes.

Butterfly the prawns/shrimp (cut down the back lengthwise with a sharp knife) and add them to the pan with the lime juice, sugar and fish sauce and simmer for 1 minute or until the prawns/shrimp are pink. Scatter the reserved coriander/cilantro leaves into the soup. Take off the heat and taste, adding more fish sauce, lime juice or sugar.

Divide the soup between 4–6 bowls and serve immediately.

simple relishes

These are four simple relishes which are lovely on soups, where their freshness contrasts against sometimes heavy vegetables. They get a bit lost on chunky soups so are best used for the puréed varieties.

tomato, chive and red onion relish

3 plum tomatoes, deseeded and finely chopped
1 tablespoon snipped chives
½ red onion, finely chopped
1 small garlic clove, crushed
3 tablespoons extra virgin olive oil

Makes 250 g/1 cup

Combine all the ingredients in a bowl and season to taste.

red pepper relish

½ red pepper, finely chopped
2 tablespoons freshly chopped coriander/cilantro
2 spring onions/scallions, sliced
freshly squeezed juice of 1 lime
1 tablespoon extra virgin olive oil

Makes 250 g/1 cup

Combine all the ingredients in a bowl and season to taste.

preserved lemon and olive relish

1 large or 3 small preserved lemons
50 g/⅓ cup pitted green olives, chopped
2 tablespoons extra virgin olive oil
2 tablespoons freshly chopped flat-leaf parsley
½ teaspoon paprika

Makes 200 g/¾ cup

Halve the preserved lemons. Scoop out the flesh and discard. Finely chop the skin and put in a bowl. Stir in the olives, olive oil and parsley (don't add any salt as the lemons are salty enough). Sprinkle the paprika over the top.

pear, date and pine nut relish

25 g/2 tablespoons butter
25 g/¼ cup pine nuts
2 pears, peeled, cored and cut into 2 cm/¾ inch cubes
3 Medjool dates, finely chopped
75 ml/⅓ cup cider vinegar
2 tablespoons dark brown soft sugar

Makes 300 g/1¼ cups

Melt the butter in a saucepan over medium heat and add the pine nuts. Cook, stirring, for about 2 minutes or until golden. Add the pears, cover and cook for 2–3 minutes until softening. Add the dates, vinegar and sugar, season and cook for a further 10–15 minutes, uncovered, until the liquid has evaporated (add a splash of water if it dries out too fast). Leave to cool a little before serving.

flavoured butters

These butters only take 10 minutes to whip together, if you remember to leave the butter out to soften! They'll make a fair bit, which you can freeze for up to 6 weeks and use on soups, simple grilled chicken or steak suppers.

garlic, coriander/cilantro and lime butter

100 g/7 tablespoons butter, softened

1 garlic clove, crushed

4 tablespoons freshly chopped coriander/cilantro

finely grated zest of 2 unwaxed limes and freshly squeezed juice of 1

Makes 115 g/1 stick

Beat the butter in a mixing bowl with a wooden spoon until light and fluffy. Add the garlic, coriander/cilantro and lime zest and juice and season well. Beat together until combined. Using a spatula, scoop out the butter and place on a 20-cm/8-inch square of parchment paper. Roll up into a sausage, twist the ends and chill for 1 hour. Slice off rounds or melt and drizzle over your hot soup.

paprika, mint and lemon butter

150 g/1 stick plus 2 tablespoons butter, softened

1 garlic clove, crushed

1 teaspoon paprika

¼–½ teaspoon dried chilli/hot pepper flakes

2 tablespoons freshly chopped mint

2 spring onions/scallions, finely chopped

finely grated zest of 1 unwaxed lemon and freshly squeezed juice of ½

Makes 165 g/1 stick plus 3 tablespoons

Beat the butter in a mixing bowl with a wooden spoon until light and fluffy. Add the garlic, paprika, chilli/hot pepper flakes, mint, spring onions/scallions, lemon zest and juice and season well. Beat together until combined. Using a spatula, scoop out the butter and place on a 20-cm/8-inch square of parchment paper. Roll up into a sausage, twist the ends and chill for 1 hour. Slice off rounds or melt and drizzle over your hot soup.

croutons etc.

Croutons add a much-needed contrast of crunch to creamy or puréed soups. A simple Apple, Parsnip and Thyme (page 45), for example, is an ideal candidate for a scattering of croutons. But really you can scatter them on anything you like.

baked croutons

90 ml/6 tablespoons extra virgin olive oil

1 garlic clove, crushed

1 small baguette or ½ large baguette, cut into 2-cm/¾-inch cubes

100 g/3½ oz. Gruyère cheese or Parmesan (optional)

Makes 15–20

Preheat the oven to 200°C (400°F) Gas 6.

Mix the oil and garlic together and season well. Place the baguette on a baking sheet and brush with the oil. If you'd like cheesy croutons, scatter over the cheese. Bake in the preheated oven for 20–25 minutes until crisp and golden.

fried garlic croutons

100 ml/⅓ cup extra virgin olive oil

3 slices of stale white bread, 2 cm/¾ inch thick (crusts cut off), cut into 2-cm/¾-inch cubes

4 whole garlic cloves, unpeeled

Makes 30–40

Heat the olive oil in a large frying pan until a bread cube sizzles and turns brown in 4 seconds. Add the bread and garlic. Cook, stirring constantly, over medium heat for 2 minutes, or until golden brown. Discard the garlic cloves and drain the croutons on paper towels.

poppy seed and garlic bagel toasts

There is no comparison between store-bought and home-made bagel toasts. They are also dead simple to make. Try them with dips or serve as part of a buffet bread basket.

3 plain bagels
3 tablespoons olive oil
2 garlic cloves, crushed
1 tablespoon poppy seeds

Serves 4

Preheat the grill/broiler to hot.

Slice each bagel into 4 and arrange on the grill/broiler pan. Grill/broil one side until brown. Remove from the heat and turn over.

Combine the oil and garlic in a bowl and brush over the untoasted side of the bagels. Scatter over the poppy seeds and return to the grill/broiler. Grill/broil until crisp and golden. Serve immediately with dips or as they are, or let cool and store in an airtight container for up to 2 days.

taleggio and sage focaccia rolls

This is very much like batch-baking bread rolls. You make individual rolls, then push them into a baking pan together, so you can break them off as you want to eat them and they stay soft on the inside.

250 g/scant 2 cups strong flour
2 teaspoons easy-blend dried yeast
1 teaspoon caster/granulated sugar
1 teaspoon salt
150 ml/⅓ cup milk, warmed
4 tablespoons extra virgin olive oil
300 g/10½ oz. Taleggio cheese (rind cut off), cubed
a handful of fresh sage leaves, roughly chopped
1 tablespoon rock salt
freshly ground black pepper

an 18-cm/7-inch square cake pan, lined with parchment paper

Makes 9

Put the flour in a food mixer with a dough hook, or in a mixing bowl.

In a separate bowl, mix together the yeast, sugar and salt and 3 tablespoons of the warm milk. Add the yeast mixture to the flour and mix, adding enough of the remaining milk and the oil to create a soft but not too sticky dough. If using a mixer, knead for 8 minutes or knead by hand on a lightly floured surface for 15 minutes until smooth and elastic. Put the dough in a clean bowl, cover and leave in a warm place for 30 minutes until doubled in size.

Roll the dough out on a lightly floured surface into a rectangle 30 x 20 cm/12 x 8 inches. Scatter with the cheese and most of the sage. Season with freshly ground black pepper. Roll up from the long side to cover all the cheese and sit on its seam. Cut into 2.5-cm/1-inch slices – you should get 9 rolls. Arrange these in the cake pan. Scatter with the reserved sage and the salt, cover the pan with clingfilm/plastic wrap and leave to rise for 30 minutes.

Preheat the oven to 200°C (400°F) Gas 6.

Bake in the preheated oven for 25 minutes, or until golden and cooked through.

red pepper scones

225 g/1¾ cups self-raising/rising flour
50 g/3½ tablespoons butter, diced
1 teaspoon baking powder
1 tablespoon freshly chopped rosemary, plus 10 small sprigs
100 g/3½ oz. roasted red bell peppers, finely chopped
1 egg
50 ml/¼ cup milk, plus extra to glaze

Makes 10–12

Preheat the oven to 220°C (425°F) Gas 7.

Mix the flour and butter in a food processor or with your fingertips until it resembles crumbs. Mix in the baking powder, chopped rosemary, a pinch of salt and the peppers. Beat the egg with the milk, then pour into the flour, stirring with a knife until you have a smooth dough. Roll out the dough on a lightly floured surface so it is at least 2 cm/¾ inches thick and cut out 5-cm/2-inch circles. Keep rerolling until you have 10–12 scones. Push the rosemary sprigs into the tops, place on a baking sheet, brush with milk and bake for 15 minutes until golden.

cornbread muffins

Cornbread made with gritty cornmeal is a real treat and it's easy because there's no need to bother with yeast.

2 fresh green chillies/chiles, deseeded
125 g/scant 1 cup cornmeal
50 g/½ cup Parmesan, grated
200 g/1⅔ cups plain/all-purpose flour
1 tablespoon baking powder
2 tablespoons caster/granulated sugar
½ teaspoon cayenne pepper
1 egg, beaten
75 g/5 tablespoons butter, melted
284 ml/1 cup plus 2 tablespoons buttermilk
3–5 tablespoons whole milk

a muffin pan, greased

Makes 9

Preheat the oven to 180°C (350°F) Gas 4.

Chop the chillies/chiles and mix with the cornmeal, Parmesan, flour, baking powder, sugar, cayenne and a large pinch of salt. In a separate bowl, beat the egg, butter and buttermilk. Stir the wet ingredients into the dry ingredients until there are no more floury pockets and add enough milk so that it becomes wet. It won't be of pouring consistency and will have to be dolloped into the pan. Don't overbeat it or you'll make the mixture tough. Spoon into the muffin pan and bake for 30 minutes until golden.

cheesy toasts

3 tablespoons full-bodied English ale

75 g/2½ oz. strong/sharp Cheddar, grated

1½ teaspoons plain/all-purpose flour

1 egg yolk

¼ teaspoon English mustard

½ teaspoon Worcestershire sauce

1 large or 2 smaller slices of sourdough or country bread

freshly ground black pepper

Serves 1

Preheat the grill/broiler.

Pour the ale into a saucepan, sprinkle over the Cheddar and flour and stir. Cook over low heat until the cheese has melted and you have a smooth sauce. Remove from the heat and beat in the egg yolk, then add the mustard and Worcestershire sauce. Season with plenty of pepper (you shouldn't need salt).

Grill/broil or toast the bread, then spread with the melted cheese and grill/broil until the top is brown and bubbling.

vegetable gratin with fresh herbs and goat cheese

A classic of French home cooking, this gratin includes a topping of tangy goat cheese. If you grow your own herbs, add whatever is on offer: savory, majoram, oregano or any other soft-leaved herb, the more the merrier. This dish is perfect, simply served with a mixed salad of lettuce and ripe tomatoes and a big basket of fresh crusty bread.

250 ml/1 cup double/heavy cream

leaves from a small bunch of fresh flat-leaf parsley, finely chopped

a small bunch of chives, snipped

a pinch of freshly grated nutmeg

75 g/2¾ oz. Gruyère cheese, grated

1.5 kg/3 lbs. 5 oz. courgettes/zucchini, very thinly sliced

150 g/5½ oz. soft goat cheese

sea salt and freshly ground black pepper

a 24-cm/9½-inch round, deep-sided baking dish, greased

Serves 4

Preheat the oven to 190°C (375°F) Gas 5.

Put the cream, parsley, chives, nutmeg, salt and pepper in a small bowl and whisk together. Add half the Gruyère.

Arrange half the courgette/zucchini slices in the prepared baking dish, sprinkle with the remaining Gruyère and season with a little salt. Top with the remaining courgette/zucchini slices, season again and pour over the cream mixture. Crumble the goat cheese over the top.

Bake in the preheated oven for 35–45 minutes, until browned. Serve immediately with a mixed salad and sliced crusty bread.

tartiflette

2 tablespoons sunflower or other light cooking oil

200 g/7 oz. smoked bacon lardons or diced smoked streaky bacon

2 large onions, thinly sliced

2 large garlic cloves, thinly sliced

700 g/1 lb. 9 oz. waxy potatoes, e.g. Desirée, well scrubbed

a sprig of fresh rosemary (optional)

1 small or ½ large Reblochon cheese (about 275 g/9¾ oz.)

150 ml/⅔ cup double/heavy cream

freshly ground black pepper

a large ovenproof dish, greased

Serves 6

Heat the oil in a large frying pan and fry the lardons until beginning to brown. Remove from the pan with a slotted spoon. Tip in the onions, stir and fry over low heat for about 20–25 minutes until they have collapsed right down and are beginning to brown. Add the garlic about 5 minutes before the end of the cooking time. Meanwhile, cut the potatoes, unpeeled, into slices about ½ cm/¼ inch thick, place in a saucepan with the sprig of rosemary, if using, and cover with cold water. Bring to the boil and boil for 2 minutes, then remove the rosemary, drain and set the potatoes aside.

Preheat the oven to 200°C (400°F) Gas 6.

Cut the Reblochon into thin slices, removing the rind if you prefer. (If you have a very mature cheese with a sticky rind, you may prefer to remove it.)

Tip half the potatoes into the baking dish, cover with half the onions and bacon and season with pepper. Repeat with the remaining potatoes, onions and bacon and pour over the cream. Distribute the Reblochon over the top of the dish, then bake in the preheated oven for 15–20 minutes until the cheese is brown and bubbling. Serve with a green salad.

ham and blue cheese gratin

This is a French recipe which traditionally calls for Gruyère cheese only, but the blue cheese used here makes it even better. There are many kinds of blue cheese and any one will do for this dish. You can also experiment with different kinds of ham; cured ham works especially well. Serve with lots of crusty bread or boiled potatoes and a green salad.

6 chicory/Belgian endive (about 90 g/3¼ oz. each)

1–2 tablespoons olive oil

12 slices smoked ham

2–3 tablespoons freshly grated Gruyère or Parmesan

sea salt

For the sauce

50 g/3½ tablespoons unsalted butter

35 g/⅓ cup plain/all-purpose flour

600 ml/2⅔ cups hot milk

½ teaspoon sea salt

½ teaspoon paprika

100 g/3½ oz. grated Gruyère

65 g/2½ oz. any firm blue cheese

a 33 x 21-cm/12½ x 8½-inch baking dish, greased

Serves 4–6

Preheat the oven to 200°C (400°F) Gas 6.

Halve the chicory lengthwise. Drizzle with the oil and rub with your hands to coat evenly. Arrange in a single layer on a baking sheet. Sprinkle lightly with salt and drizzle over 4 tablespoons water. Roast in the preheated oven for about 15 minutes, until just tender when pierced with a knife. Remove from the oven and let cool. Leave the oven on.

Meanwhile, prepare the béchamel. Melt the butter in a heavy-based saucepan. Stir in the flour and cook, stirring constantly, for 1 minute. Pour in the hot milk gradually, whisking constantly and continue whisking gently for 3–5 minutes, until the sauce begins to thicken. Season with salt and paprika and add both the cheeses. Stir to combine.

As soon as the chicory are cool enough to handle, carefully wrap each one with a slice of ham and arrange them side-by-side, seam-side down, in the prepared baking dish. Pour over the béchamel, spreading evenly to coat. Sprinkle with the grated cheese and bake in the still hot oven for about 20–30 minutes, until browned and bubbling. Serve immediately with a leafy green salad and crusty bread.

salmon, broccoli and potato gratin with pesto

This can be prepared the night or morning before serving. Simply assemble the gratin, up to the point of pouring on the cream, cover and refrigerate.

975 g/2 lbs. 3 oz. waxy potatoes, peeled

a large head of broccoli (about 480 g/1 lb. 1 oz.), separated into florets

400 g/14 oz. boneless, skinless salmon fillet

1 tablespoon olive oil

20 g/½ cup fresh breadcrumbs

4 tablespoons freshly grated Parmesan

250 ml/1 cup single/light cream

2 tablespoons fresh pesto

4 tablespoons milk

2–3 tablespoons butter, cut into small pieces

sea salt and freshly ground black pepper

a 30 x 20-cm/12 x 8-inch baking dish, greased

Serves 4–6

Preheat the oven to 200°C (400°F) Gas 6.

Put the potatoes in a large saucepan and add sufficient cold water to cover. Parboil until almost tender when pierced with a knife. Drain. When cool enough to handle slice into ½-cm/¼-inch thick rounds.

Bring another saucepan of water to the boil. Add the broccoli and a pinch of salt and cook for 3–4 minutes, until tender. Drain and let cool. Cut into pieces and set aside.

Rub the salmon fillets with the oil and place on a sheet of kitchen foil, turned up at the sides to catch any juices, and put it on a baking sheet. Sprinkle with a little salt. Bake in the preheated oven for about 10–15 minutes, until cooked through. Let cool, then flake, removing any small bones and set aside.

In a small bowl, mix together the breadcrumbs and 2 tablespoons of the Parmesan. Season well and set aside. In another bowl, stir together the cream and pesto. Season well and set aside.

To assemble, arrange the potato slices on the bottom of the prepared baking dish in an even layer, sprinkle with salt, the remaining Parmesan and drizzle with the milk. Arrange the broccoli in an even layer on top of the potatoes and season lightly. Top with the cooked salmon in an even layer.

Pour over the pesto and cream mixture. Sprinkle the breadcrumb mixture over the top and dot with butter. Bake in the preheated oven for 25–30 minutes, until just browned. Serve immediately.

mashed potato pie with bacon, leeks and cheese

This is a great way to make a meal out of simple mashed potato. Bacon, leeks and cheese make a particularly perfect trio, but you can add just about anything to this versatile dish. You should have onion at the very least, and cheese of some sort, and something green for a bit of colour, after that anything goes!

1 kg/2 lbs. 4 oz. floury potatoes
2 tablespoons olive oil
1 onion, finely chopped
2 small leeks, thinly sliced
80 g/3 oz. bacon or pancetta, diced
30 g/2 tablespoons butter
250 ml/1 cup milk or single/light cream (or a bit of both)
1 egg, beaten
a large handful of fresh parsley leaves, chopped
a pinch of paprika
90 g/3¼ oz. firm cheese, such as Gruyère, grated
sea salt and freshly ground
black pepper

a 24-cm/9½-inch round baking dish, greased

Serves 4–6

Halve or quarter the potatoes depending on their size; they should be about the same to cook evenly. Put them in a large saucepan, add sufficient cold water to cover, salt well and bring to the boil. Simmer for 20 minutes, until tender.

Meanwhile, heat the oil in a frying pan over low heat. Add the onion and leeks and cook gently for about 10 minutes, until soft. Add the bacon and cook for 3–5 minutes, until just browned. Season with salt and set aside.

Preheat the oven to 190°C (375°F) Gas 5.

Drain the potatoes and mash coarsely, mixing in the butter and milk. Season well and add the egg. Stir to combine.

Stir in the leek mixture, parsley, paprika and half the cheese. Transfer to the prepared dish and spread evenly. Sprinkle over the remaining cheese and bake in the preheated oven for 35–45 minutes, until well browned. Serve immediately.

smoked trout hash with horseradish cream

A perfect supper dish for two which is speedy to make and satisfying to eat. It could almost be accused of being too simple but the horseradish cream dresses it up nicely. This really is a meal in itself, but you could serve with crusty bread and a peppery watercress salad.

500 g/1 lb. 2 oz. baby new potatoes, scrubbed
30 g/2 tablespoons unsalted butter
2–3 tablespoons olive oil
1 small red onion, finely chopped
1 celery stalk, finely chopped
½ teaspoon paprika
1 tablespoon chopped fresh dill
1 tablespoon grated lemon zest
250 g/9 oz. smoked trout, cut in pieces
sea salt and freshly ground black pepper
lemon wedges, to serve

Horseradish cream
4–5 tablespoons sour cream or plain yogurt
2 teaspoons creamed horseradish
a small bunch of fresh chives, snipped

Serves 2

Put the potatoes in a large saucepan with sufficient water to cover. Add a pinch of salt and boil until tender when pierced with a knife. Drain. When cool enough to handle, cut into cubes.

Meanwhile, make the horseradish cream. Combine the sour cream, horseradish and chives in a bowl. Mix, cover and set aside.

Melt the butter and 1 tablespoon of the oil in a large frying pan. Add the cubed potatoes with a pinch of salt and cook, stirring occasionally, for about 10 minutes, until browned. Add the onion, celery, paprika, dill and lemon zest to the pan and cook, stirring occasionally, for 5 minutes more. Stir in the trout, season, and add a little more oil if the mixture seems dry. Continue cooking, turning every so often, until the hash is well browned.

Serve immediately with the horseradish cream for spooning and lemon wedges.

Variation: Replace the smoked trout with chopped bacon or ham, omit the lemon zest and use parsley in place of the dill. For a vegetarian version, replace the bacon with diced green pepper. Serve either variation with a fried egg on top and a dash of Tabasco can replace the horseradish.

saffron risotto with aged parmesan, sage and serrano ham

A good risotto depends on good ingredients, so make sure you have a well-flavoured stock, good-quality ham and well-aged Parmesan (or Grana Padano) cheese.

600 ml/2⅓ cups chicken stock

40 g/2½ tablespoons butter

1 small onion or ½ medium onion, finely chopped

175 g/⅔ cup arborio or other Italian risotto rice

½ glass (about 75 ml/⅓ cup) dry white wine

a Parmesan rind (optional)

a small pinch (about ¼ teaspoon) saffron strands

1–2 tablespoons jellied meat juices* (optional)

25 g/1 oz. aged Parmesan, freshly grated, plus a few Parmesan shavings

2 tablespoons olive oil

2–3 slices of Serrano or other Spanish air-dried ham, each torn into 3

8–10 fresh sage leaves

sea salt and freshly ground black pepper

* The meat juices which collect under the fat you pour off when cooking a chicken or a pork joint.

Serves 2

Bring the stock to the boil, then leave it simmering on a low heat. Melt 25 g/1½ tablespoons of the butter over medium heat in a large saucepan, add the onion and cook gently for about 5 minutes, until soft. Tip in the rice, stir and cook for 2–3 minutes until the grains have turned opaque and are beginning to catch on the bottom of the pan. Add the wine, stir and let it bubble up and evaporate.

Add the Parmesan rind if you have one, then begin to add the hot stock, adding about a coffee cup at a time and allowing the liquid to be absorbed by the rice before you add the next lot. Cook for about 20 minutes, stirring regularly, until the rice begins to look creamy but still has some bite to it. Pour the last bit of stock over the saffron and add to the risotto along with a couple of spoonfuls of jellied meat juices, if using. Turn off the heat, add the remaining butter and the grated Parmesan and stir. Cover the pan and let the flavours amalgamate for 2–3 minutes.

Heat the oil in a frying pan and quickly fry the ham. Remove from the pan with a slotted spoon and drain on paper towels. Fry the sage leaves in the same pan until crisp. Give the risotto a final stir and season to taste. Serve immediately, topped with the crisp ham, sage leaves and a few shavings of Parmesan.

barley risotto with mushrooms and goat cheese

Barley makes an interesting substitute for rice in a risotto. It has a nutty and sweet flavour which works well here with both the mushrooms, the red wine and the goat cheese

20 g/1 oz. dried porcini mushrooms

1 litre/4 cups vegetable stock

65 ml/⅓ cup red wine

50 g/3½ tablespoons butter

1 tablespoon olive oil

1 leek, trimmed and thinly sliced

2 garlic cloves, chopped

330 g/scant 2 cups pearl barley

400 g/4 cups fresh brown mushrooms, sliced

50 g/¼ cup soft goat cheese

a small handful of fresh flat-leaf parsley leaves, finely chopped

sea salt and freshly ground black pepper.

Serves 4

Put the dried mushrooms in a heatproof bowl and cover with 125 ml/½ cup boiling water. Let soak for 20 minutes. Drain the mushrooms and reserve the soaking liquid. Roughly chop the mushrooms and set aside.

Combine the stock, red wine and reserved mushroom-soaking liquid in a saucepan over low heat.

Heat half of the butter and the oil in a heavy-based saucepan over medium heat. Add the leek and garlic and cook for about 4–5 minutes, until the leek has softened. Stir in the barley and cook for 1 minute, until glossy.

Stir in the fresh and dried mushrooms and cook for 2–3 minutes, until the mushrooms have wilted.

Add about 125 ml/½ cup of the hot stock mixture to the barley and stir constantly, until almost all the liquid has been absorbed. (This will take a little longer than cooking with risotto rice.) Continue adding the liquid a little at a time and stirring for about 45 minutes, until all the liquid has been added and the barley is tender.

Stir in the goat cheese and remaining butter, until the cheese has melted. Season to taste with salt and pepper and sprinkle over the parsley. Serve immediately.

fireside feasts

Home-cooked comforts
such as casseroles, bakes,
pies, roasts and stews are
ideal for winter entertaining.
With something delicious
bubbling on the stove, your
guests will be delighted
as they come in from
the cold.

tuna noodle casserole

This hearty all-American favourite is brought up to date with a delicious, freshly-made sauce using mushrooms and capers. This recipe makes a perfect mid-week family meal served with a generous and colourful salad.

2 tablespoons olive oil

3 spring onions/scallions, thinly sliced

1 celery stalk, finely chopped

100 g/scant 1 cup button mushrooms, halved and thinly sliced

2 tablespoons capers (optional)

150 g/3 cups fresh breadcrumbs

a good pinch of paprika

350 g/12 oz. dried egg tagliatelle

50 g/3½ tablespoons unsalted butter

35 g/⅓ cup plain/all-purpose flour

600 ml/2⅓ cups hot milk

1 teaspoon mustard powder

350-g/12-oz. can tuna in oil, drained and flaked

a large handful of fresh parsley leaves, chopped

sea salt and freshly ground black pepper

a 30 x 20-cm/12 x 8-inch baking dish, greased

Serves 4

Preheat the oven to 180°C (350°F) Gas 4.

Heat the oil in a large frying pan and add the spring onions/scallions, celery and mushrooms. Cook over medium heat for 3–5 minutes, until soft. Season lightly with salt, stir in the capers (if using) and set aside. Season the breadcrumbs and add the paprika. Set aside.

Cook the pasta according to the manufacturer's instructions. Drain, toss in a little olive oil and set aside.

Melt the butter in a small saucepan set over low heat. Add the flour and cook, stirring, for 1 minute. Gradually pour in the hot milk, whisking constantly, and simmer until the mixture thickens. Stir in the mustard. Let cool slightly. Taste and adjust the seasoning if necessary.

Put the cooked pasta in the prepared baking dish. Pour over the sauce, mushroom mixture, tuna and parsley and toss to mix well. Spread evenly and sprinkle the seasoned breadcrumbs over the top. Bake in the preheated oven for 20–30 minutes, until browned. Serve immediately with a mixed salad.

extra-crispy macaroni cheese

The best bit about macaroni cheese, as we all know, is the crispy topping. Imagine how wonderful it would be to have crispy bits all the way through. It is very easy, and this is how you do it.

125–150 g/4½–5 oz. mature/sharp Cheddar, coarsely grated

25 g/2 tablespoons butter

25 g/3 tablespoons plain/all-purpose flour

300 ml/1¼ cups whole milk

175 g/6 oz. rigatoni or penne

½ teaspoon English mustard or 1 teaspoon Dijon mustard

a few drops of Worcestershire sauce

sea salt and freshly ground black pepper

a shallow ovenproof dish, greased

Serves 2–3

Preheat the oven to 170°C (325°F) Gas 3.

Sprinkle 50 g/1¾ oz. of the Cheddar in an even layer over a baking sheet. Bake in the preheated oven for 8–10 minutes until bubbling and beginning to brown. Remove from the oven, leave to cool, then break into pieces.

Put the butter in a medium non-stick saucepan and melt gently. Stir in the flour and cook for a few seconds, then take the pan off the heat and add the milk little by little, stirring before you add the next amount. Put the pan back on the hob, increase the heat slightly, then bring the sauce gradually to the boil, stirring continuously. Turn the heat right down again and leave the sauce to simmer for 5 minutes, stirring it occasionally.

Bring a large saucepan of water to the boil, add salt, then tip in the pasta. Cook according to the manufacturer's instructions. Meanwhile, preheat the grill/broiler.

Just before the pasta is ready, stir half the remaining Cheddar into the sauce, add the mustard and Worcestershire sauce and season to taste. Add a little more milk if it looks too thick.

Drain the pasta thoroughly and tip into the prepared ovenproof dish. Scatter the crispy cheese pieces over the pasta and mix together. Pour in the cheese sauce, then sprinkle over the remaining Cheddar. Place the dish under the hot grill/broiler for about 5 minutes until the top is brown and crispy.

artichoke, mushroom and olive pasta bake with provolone

2–3 tablespoons olive oil

1 onion, finely chopped

½ teaspoon dried oregano

½ teaspoon dried thyme

130 g/1 cup white mushrooms, chopped

4 garlic cloves, crushed

¼ teaspoon dried chilli/hot pepper flakes

125 ml/½ cup dry white or red wine

2 x 400-g/14-oz. cans chopped tomatoes

1 x 400-g/14-oz. can artichoke hearts, drained and sliced

50 g/⅓ cup pitted black olives, sliced

a pinch of sugar

400 g/14 oz. dried tube pasta

150 g/5½ oz. provolone, cubed

Béchamel sauce

50 g/3½ tablespoons unsalted butter

35 g/4¼ tablespoons plain/all-purpose flour

600 ml/2⅓ cups hot milk

3–4 tablespoons freshly grated Parmesan

sea salt and freshly ground black pepper

a 30 x 20-cm/12 x 8-inch baking dish

Serves 4

Heat 1 tablespoon of the oil in a large frying pan. Add the onion and cook over low heat for about 5 minutes, until soft. Stir in the oregano, thyme and mushrooms and cook for 2–3 minutes more, adding a little more oil if required. Stir in the garlic and dried chilli/hot pepper flakes and season with salt. Cook for 1 minute, then add the wine. Cook for 1 minute more, then add the tomatoes, artichokes and olives. Add the sugar, season, stir to combine and simmer for about 15 minutes. Taste and adjust the seasoning if necessary.

Preheat the oven to 200°C (400°F) Gas 6.

To prepare the béchamel sauce, melt the butter in a heavy-based saucepan set over low heat. Add the flour and cook, stirring, for 1 minute. Slowly pour in the hot milk, whisking continuously, and simmer until the mixture thickens. Season well. Stir in 2 tablespoons of the Parmesan and set aside. Cook the pasta according the manufacturer's instructions until just al dente. Drain and set aside.

To assemble, spread a small amount of the tomato mixture over the bottom of the baking dish and add 1 tablespoon of the oil. Arrange one-third of the cooked pasta in a single layer on top of the tomato. Top with half of the remaining tomato mixture and spread evenly. Cover with another layer of pasta (using half of the remaining amount). Spoon over half of the béchamel and spread evenly. Top with the provolone. Spoon the remaining tomato mixture on top. Top with the remaining pasta and béchamel. Sprinkle with the remaining Parmesan. Bake in the preheated oven for about 30–40 minutes, until browned. Serve immediately.

sausage, pasta and bean stew with greens

Easy to make and even easier to enjoy, this is truly a one-pot meal. It can be served as soon as the sausage and pasta are cooked, which doesn't take long at all, but the taste improves if made in advance. If using spicy sausage, you may not need to add the dried chilli/hot pepper flakes. Serve with a basket of crusty bread and offer extra finely grated Parmesan for sprinkling.

1 tablespoon olive oil

1 large onion, coarsely chopped

12 Italian- or Toulouse-style sausages (about 800 g/1 lb. 12 oz.) cut into bite-sized pieces

4 garlic cloves, sliced

¼–1 teaspoon dried chilli/hot pepper flakes, to taste

400-g/14-oz. can chopped tomatoes

250 ml/1 cup red wine

1 bay leaf

100 g/3½ oz. small pasta shapes, such as macaroni

about 175 g/1¾ cups greens, such as curly kale, chard or cavolo nero

1 x 400-g/14-oz. can cannellini beans, drained

a large handful of fresh basil leaves, chopped

sea salt and freshly ground black pepper

freshly grated Parmesan, to serve

Serves 4–6

Heat the oil in a large saucepan. Add the onion and cook for 3–5 minutes, until soft. Add the sausage and cook for about 5 minutes, until browned. Stir in the garlic and dried chilli/hot pepper flakes and cook for 1 minute.

Add the tomatoes, wine and bay leaf and enough water to cover. Don't worry if it's soupy at this stage. Bring to the boil, then add the pasta and cook, uncovered, for about 10 minutes, until the pasta is al dente.

Meanwhile bring a separate large saucepan of lightly salted water to the boil. Add the greens and cook briefly just to blanch. Drain and set aside.

Add the blanched greens and beans to the sausage mixture and stir well. Simmer, uncovered, for a further 5 minutes. Taste and adjust the seasoning. Stir in the basil and serve sprinkled with finely grated Parmesan and plenty of crusty bread on the side.

chicken pot pie with tarragon and leeks

1 tablespoon olive oil

1 tablespoon butter

1 onion, chopped

2 carrots, sliced

2 trimmed leeks, sliced

a splash of dry white wine

60 g/⅔ cup button mushrooms, quartered

500 g/1 lb. 2 oz. cooked chicken, cut into bite-sized pieces

75 g/½ cup frozen peas

375 g/13 oz. ready-rolled puff pastry, defrosted if frozen

a little beaten egg, for glazing

sea salt and freshly ground black pepper

For the sauce

50 g/3½ tablespoons butter

35 g/4¼ tablespoons plain/all-purpose flour

500 ml/2 cups hot chicken stock

100 ml/⅓ cup single/light cream

several sprigs of fresh tarragon, leaves stripped and chopped

a small bunch of fresh chives, snipped

leaves from a small bunch of fresh parsley, finely chopped

a 30 x 20-cm/12 x 8-inch baking dish

Serves 4–6

Preheat the oven to 190°C (375°F) Gas 5.

Heat the oil and butter in a large non-stick frying pan. Add the onion, carrots and leeks and cook, stirring occasionally, for 5–8 minutes, until soft. Season well with salt and pepper, add the mushrooms and wine, if using, and cook for 3–5 minutes more. You may need to add a drop more oil or butter. Add the chicken and peas, and set aside.

To make the sauce, melt the butter in a heavy-based saucepan set over low heat. Add the flour and cook for 1 minute, stirring continuously. Slowly pour in the hot stock and cream, whisking continuously, and simmer until the mixture thickens. Season well. Stir in the tarragon, chives and parsley. Taste and adjust the seasoning if necessary.

Transfer the chicken mixture to the baking dish and pour over the sauce. Mix to combine.

Unroll the pastry on a lightly floured surface. Lay the sheet on top of the filling, crimping the edges to sit just inside the edge and trimming off any excess with a sharp knife (you can use the trimmings for decoration, if liked). Cut an 'X' in the middle to allow steam to escape and brush with the beaten egg. Bake in the preheated oven for 30–40 minutes, until golden brown. Serve immediately.

Variation: For a vegetarian version, omit the chicken and use vegetable stock. Increase the carrot, leek and mushroom quantities slightly and add about 300 g/10½ oz. of any one (or a combination) of the following vegetables which has been cooked and cubed where appropriate: swede, turnip, parsnip, broccoli and/or cauliflower florets, courgettes/zucchini, green beans or asparagus.

steak, leek and mushroom pie with Guinness

Pies are a wonderful thing. They look and taste fantastic, and are really straightforward to make, especially if you leave out the bottom layer of pastry, which I always do. Serve with plenty of creamy mashed potatoes and peas.

1 tablespoon vegetable oil

700 g/1 lb. 9 oz. stewing beef, cut into bite-sized pieces

2 trimmed leeks, sliced

1 onion, coarsely chopped

2 large carrots, peeled and diced

250 g/2½ cups mushrooms, coarsely chopped

100 g/3½ oz. bacon (about 3 rashers), coarsely chopped

1 teaspoon dried thyme

2 garlic cloves, crushed

2 tablespoons plain/all-purpose flour

330-ml/11 oz. can Guinness

2 tablespoons Worcestershire sauce

1 bay leaf

a large handful of fresh parsley leaves, chopped

375 g/13 oz. ready-rolled puff pastry, defrosted if frozen

melted butter or milk, to brush

sea salt and freshly ground black pepper

a large flameproof casserole

a 30 x 20-cm/12 x 8-inch baking dish

Serves 4–6

Preheat the oven to 160°C (325°F) Gas 3.

Heat the oil in a heatproof casserole dish. Add the beef and cook, stirring, for 2–3 minutes, until browned. Remove the meat from the casserole dish, season and set aside.

Add the leeks, onion and carrots to the pan, adding a little more oil if necessary. Cook over low heat for about 3 minutes, until softened. Add the mushrooms, bacon and thyme and cook for a further 2–3 minutes. Season well. Add the garlic and cook for 1 minute.

Return the beef to the casserole dish, add the flour, stir to coat the meat in the flour and cook for 2–3 minutes. Pour in the Guinness and Worcestershire sauce. Add the bay leaf and parsley and pour in sufficient cold water to just cover. Stir to mix, cover with a lid and bake in the preheated oven for about 1½ hours.

Remove the casserole dish from the oven and increase the oven temperature to 200°C (400°F) Gas 6.

Transfer the beef mixture to the baking dish. Unroll the pastry and use to cover the pie filling. It should look rustic, so fold over the edges and crimp roughly with your fingers. Using a sharp knife, and starting at the top edge, make lengthwise slits on the diagonal, in stripes about ½ cm apart, all the way across. Brush with melted butter or milk and bake in the preheated oven for about 25–30 minutes, until golden. Serve immediately with mashed potatoes and peas on the side.

Moroccan chicken pie

Ideal for large gatherings or buffets, this is best when made in advance giving the flavours time to mingle. The filling can also be made into individual pies or pastries. Serve with a grated carrot salad and plenty of buttery couscous.

2 tablespoons olive oil

1 onion, grated

1 teaspoon ground cinnamon

2 teaspoons ground ginger

½ teaspoon turmeric

a pinch of saffron threads

1 teaspoon paprika

½ teaspoon ground cumin

½ teaspoon ground black pepper

1 garlic clove, crushed

8 chicken thighs, skin removed

40 g/¼ cup raisins

35 g/½ cup flaked almonds

a large handful of fresh coriander/cilantro leaves, chopped

1 tablespoon freshly squeezed lemon juice

270 g/9¾ oz. ready made filo/phyllo pastry

2–3 tablespoons butter, melted

sea salt and freshly ground black pepper

a 24-cm/9½-inch round baking dish or tart pan, greased

Serves 4–6

Heat the oil in a large saucepan over low heat. Add the onion and cook for 5–8 minutes, until just soft. Stir in the spices and garlic and cook for 1 minute. Add the chicken and stir to coat in the spiced oil. Add 190 ml/¾ cup water and the raisins. Season generously with salt. Bring to the boil, reduce the heat, cover and simmer for about 20–30 minutes, until the chicken is cooked through. Set aside.

Preheat the oven to 190°C (375°F) Gas 5.

When the chicken is cool enough to handle, shred the meat and discard the bones. Return the meat to the cooking juices. Mix well, taste and adjust the seasoning. The mixture should be very moist but it should not be soupy. If there is a lot of liquid, return to the heat and cook to reduce slightly. Stir in the almonds, coriander/cilantro and lemon juice. Set aside.

To assemble, place 2 sheets of filo/phyllo on the work surface. Using the baking dish, cut out 2 circles of pastry to fit. Cover with a clean, damp dish towel and set aside. Line the sides of the dish with the remaining pastry, positioning each one with an overhang and not quite reaching the middle. Continue until the edge is covered with overhanging sheets of filo/phyllo. Brush the dish with melted butter and top with one of the pastry circles. Brush with more butter and top with the remaining circle.

Transfer the chicken mixture to the filo/phyllo-lined dish, spreading it evenly. Fold in the overhanging filo to part-enclose the filling, crinkling it as you go. Brush with melted butter. Bake in the preheated oven for 30–40 minutes, until just golden. Serve warm or at room temperature.

smoked haddock and potato gratin

This may sound and look rustic but the taste is very sophisticated, making it an ideal choice for when you need to cook something elegant yet easy. Use good-quality undyed smoked haddock fillet for best results. Serve the gratin with sautéed green beans or, if you are serving it as a midweek meal, then a green salad is all that's required.

1.5 kg/3 lbs. 5 oz. potatoes

1 bay leaf

15 g/½ cup dried wild mushrooms

1 onion, chopped

2 tablespoons olive oil

150 g/1½ cups white mushrooms, sliced

125 ml/½ cup dry white wine

280 g/10 oz. undyed smoked haddock fillet, shredded, bones removed

a large handful of fresh flat-leaf parsley leaves, chopped

265 ml/1 cup plus 1 tablespoon single/light cream

250 ml/1 cup milk

2 tablespoons butter, melted

sea salt and freshly ground black pepper

a 33 x 21-cm/13 x 8½-inch oval baking dish, greased

Serves 4–6

Put the potatoes in a large saucepan, add the bay leaf and add sufficient cold water to cover well. Parboil until almost tender when pierced with a knife. Drain. When cool enough to handle, slice into ½-cm/¼-inch thick rounds.

Put the dried mushrooms in a heatproof bowl and add sufficient boiling water to cover. Soak for about 15 minutes, until soft. Discard all but 2 tablespoons of the soaking liquid. Drain the mushrooms, chop coarsely and set aside.

Preheat the oven to 200°C (400°F) Gas 6.

Put 1 tablespoon of the oil in a large frying pan and add the onion. Cook for 3–5 minutes, until soft. Add the white mushrooms and the remaining oil and season well. Cook, stirring, for 3–5 minutes, until the mushrooms begin to brown. Add the wine and reserved mushroom soaking liquid and cook for 1 minute. Stir in the dried mushrooms, haddock and parsley and cook for 2–3 minutes.

Combine the cream and milk in a small bowl or jug/pitcher, season and set aside.

To assemble, arrange half the potato slices on the bottom of the prepared dish (save the most even and attractive slices for the top layer). Sprinkle lightly with salt. Spread the fish mixture in an even layer on top of the potatoes. Top with the remaining potatoes, arranged neatly. Sprinkle lightly with salt, then pour over the cream mixture. Brush the top with melted butter and bake in the preheated oven for about 1–1½ hours, until golden. Serve immediately.

tamale pie

This deliciously spicy pie with its golden cornbread topping will warm you up on a cold winter's night. Serve with sour cream and a salad of thinly sliced tomatoes and onions, dressed with oil, lime juice and a sprinkling of chopped fresh coriander/cilantro.

1 tablespoon vegetable oil

1 onion, finely chopped

1 green pepper, finely chopped

500 g/1 lb. minced/ground pork or beef

2 teaspoons chilli/chili powder

1 teaspoon ground cumin

½ teaspoon cayenne pepper (optional)

½ teaspoon allspice

400-g/14-oz. can kidney beans or black beans, drained

400-g/14-oz. can chopped tomatoes

100 g/½ cup pitted black olives, sliced

150 g/1 cup corn kernels, canned or frozen

1 tablespoon Worcestershire sauce

Tabasco sauce (optional)

sea salt and freshly ground black pepper

For the topping

300 g/1 cup plain/all-purpose flour

300 g/1 cup cornmeal

2 teaspoons baking powder

¼ teaspoon salt

a pinch of sugar

3 tablespoons melted butter

180 ml/¾ cup milk or buttermilk

1 egg, beaten

1 small fresh green chilli/chile, very finely chopped

45 g/½ cup grated Cheddar

a 30 x 20-cm/12 x 8-inch baking dish

Serves 4–6

Preheat the oven to 190°C (375°F) Gas 5.

Heat the oil in a frying pan. Add the onion and green pepper and cook for about 5 minutes, until soft. Season and add the meat, chilli/chili powder, cumin, cayenne and allspice. Cook, stirring often, until browned.

Stir in the beans, tomatoes, olives, sweetcorn and Worcestershire sauce. Reduce the heat and simmer, uncovered, for about 10–15 minutes.

Meanwhile, prepare the topping. Put the flour, cornmeal, baking powder, salt and sugar in a bowl and stir to combine. Stir in the melted butter, milk and egg and stir just until blended. Stir in the chilli/chile and cheese. Add an extra spoonful of milk if the mixture seems dry.

Taste the meat mixture and adjust the seasoning if necessary. Add some Tabasco if it is not hot enough. Spoon into the baking dish and spread evenly. Drop the cornmeal mixture in spoonfuls on top, spreading evenly to cover.

Bake in the preheated oven for about 30 minutes, until the topping is golden brown. Serve immediately.

Variation: For a vegetarian version, replace the meat with an additional can of beans and add 1–2 diced courgettes/zucchini, cooked along with the onion and pepper.

fish pie with leeks and herbs

1 kg/2¼ lbs. floury potatoes, peeled

2 bay leaves

115 g/1 stick unsalted butter

about 850 ml/3⅓ cups milk (250 ml/1 cup of which is warmed)

1 tablespoon olive oil

1 leek, sliced

2 tablespoons dry white wine

300 g/10 oz. any firm white fish fillet, such as cod

200 g/7 oz. boneless, skinless salmon

150 g/6 oz. undyed smoked haddock

175 g/6 oz. peeled cooked prawns/shrimp

35 g/⅓ plain/all-purpose flour

1 teaspoon dry mustard powder

a small bunch of chives, snipped

a large handful of fresh parsley leaves, chopped

sea salt and freshly ground black pepper

a 30 x 20-cm/12 x 8-inch baking dish, greased

Serves 6

Put the potatoes in a large saucepan and add sufficient cold water to cover. Add 1 of the bay leaves, season with salt and bring to the boil. Cook until the potatoes are tender when pierced with a knife. Drain well. Working in batches, mash the potatoes with all but 50 g/3 tablespoons of the butter, the 250 ml/1 cup warmed milk and some salt. Repeat until all the potatoes are mashed. Taste and adjust the seasoning. The mixture should be slightly thinner than ordinary mash to allow for baking. Set aside.

Preheat the oven to 190°C (375°F) Gas 5.

Put the oil in a small saucepan and add the leek. Cook for about 5 minutes, until soft. Season lightly, add the wine and cook until the liquid is almost fully reduced. Set aside.

Combine the remaining milk and bay leaf in a large shallow pan and bring to the boil. Add the white fish fillets and poach for about 5 minutes, until almost cooked. Transfer to a plate with a slotted spoon and season lightly. Add the salmon and repeat. Add the smoked haddock and repeat. Transfer the poaching milk to a measuring jug/pitcher; if it is not 600 ml/2½ cups, top it up with more milk.

Melt the remaining butter in a saucepan set over low heat. Add the flour and cook, whisking, for 1 minute. Slowly pour in the reserved milk, whisking continuously, and simmer until the mixture thickens. Add the mustard and season to taste. Stir in the chives and parsley.

Break the fish into pieces and put in the prepared dish. Add the prawns/shrimp and leeks. Pour over the sauce and stir well to mix. Spread evenly. Top with the mash and spread in an even layer.

Bake the pie in the preheated oven for 35–45 minutes, or until browned and bubbling up around the edges. Serve immediately.

braised pot roast with red wine, rosemary and bay leaves

This is the sort of food that makes you long for cold wintry days, when it is nice to stay indoors and simmer something slowly – heating the kitchen and filling the house with rich, warming aromas. It also has appeal for the lazy spendthrift as preparation is minimal and the cut of meat is inexpensive. Serve with creamy mashed potatoes, soft polenta or even macaroni baked in cream with Parmesan.

1.2 kg/3 lbs. braising joint, such as beef brisket, tied

2 tablespoons olive oil

1 onion, halved and thinly sliced

2 celery stalks, thinly sliced

1 large carrot, sliced

4 garlic cloves, peeled and sliced

150 g/6 oz. pancetta, very finely chopped

750 ml/3 cups robust red wine, preferably Italian

400-g/14-oz. can chopped tomatoes

1 bay leaf, 2 large sprigs fresh rosemary, several sprigs fresh parsley, all firmly tied together in a bundle

3–4 tablespoons capers in brine, drained (optional)

sea salt and freshly ground black pepper

a large heatproof casserole dish

Serves 6

Preheat the oven to 180°C (350°F) Gas 4.

Heat the oil in a large heatproof casserole dish. Add the beef and cook for about 8–10 minutes, until browned on all sides. Transfer the beef to a plate, season all over with salt and set aside.

Add the onion, celery and carrot to the casserole dish and cook, stirring often, until browned. Add the garlic and pancetta and cook for 1 minute. Season, then add the wine and tomatoes and bring to the boil. Boil for 1 minute, then add the herb bundle. Return the browned beef to the casserole dish.

Cover and transfer to the preheated oven. After 1½ hours, remove the casserole dish from the oven and turn the beef over. Pour in some water if the liquid has reduced too much and add the capers, if using. Return to the oven and cook for a further 1½ hours, until the meat is tender.

Serve in slices with the sauce and vegetables spooned over the top and with the accompaniment of your choice.

spicy pork stew with sweet potatoes and beans

The combination of sweet potato and chilli/chile here is fantastic, and it goes well with the melting texture of the pork. Like any stew, this improves with age but is flavoursome enough to serve the same day it was made. Crusty bread makes a good accompaniment.

2 tablespoons olive oil

1 large onion, chopped

2 teaspoons ground cumin

1½ teaspoons dried oregano

700 g/1½ lbs. pork shoulder, cubed

1 teaspoon clear honey

1 teaspoon ground cinnamon

2 garlic cloves, finely chopped

1 fresh red chilli/chile, sliced

400-g/14-oz. can chopped tomatoes

500 ml/2 cups chicken or vegetable stock

2–3 sweet potatoes (about 800 g/1¾ lbs.), peeled and cubed

1 bay leaf

400-g/14-oz. can kidney beans, drained

a large handful of fresh coriander/cilantro leaves, chopped

sea salt and freshly ground black pepper

plain yogurt, to serve (optional)

Serves 4

Preheat the oven to 150°C (300°F) Gas 2.

Heat 1 tablespoon of the oil in a large heatproof casserole dish. Add the onion and cook for 3–5 minutes until soft. Stir in 1 teaspoon of the cumin and the oregano and cook for 2–3 minutes until fragrant. Remove from the casserole dish and set aside.

Add the pork and the remaining oil and cook for 5–7 minutes, until browned. Stir in the honey, the remaining cumin, the cinnamon, garlic and chilli/chile. Season with salt and mix well. Return the onions to the pan and add the tomatoes, stock, sweet potatoes and bay leaf. Bring to the boil, then cover and transfer to the preheated oven. Cook for 40 minutes.

Remove from the oven and stir in the beans. Cover and return to the oven to cook for a further 20 minutes. Sprinkle with coriander/cilantro and serve with yogurt on the side, if liked, and crusty bread.

Variation: For a vegetarian version, omit the pork and add 1 diced butternut squash with the sweet potatoes and a 400-g/14-oz. can butter beans with the kidney beans. Cook in the oven for 15 minutes instead of 40 minutes.

farmhouse chicken casserole with carrots, leeks and potato

This is the perfect dish to prepare on a chilly Sunday evening to provide a meal or two during the week. You will need a good-sized casserole dish, large enough to take the chicken in a single layer.

2–3 tablespoons olive oil

1 small chicken (about 600 g/1¼ lbs.), cut into pieces, plus 4 chicken thighs

600 g/1¼ lbs. carrots, sliced thickly

500 g/1 lb. leeks, sliced

800 g/1¾ lbs. small new potatoes, cut lengthwise into wedges

a few sprigs each of fresh thyme and parsley and a bay leaf, tied firmly into a bundle with string

sea salt and freshly ground black pepper

To serve

200 ml/¾ cup single/light cream

2 tablespoons wholegrain Dijon mustard

a large handful of fresh parsley leaves, chopped

a bunch of fresh chives, snipped (optional)

a large heatproof casserole dish

Serves 6–8

Preheat the oven to 150°C (300°F) Gas 2.

Heat 2 tablespoons of the oil in a casserole dish set over medium heat. Add the chicken pieces, skin-side down, and cook for 4–5 minutes on each side, until browned. Transfer to a dish and season with salt. Cover and set aside.

If there is a lot of fat in the casserole dish drain some of it off, leaving just enough to brown the vegetables. Add the carrots and leeks and cook for 5–7 minutes, stirring occasionally, until just browned. Add the potatoes and herbs and cook for a further 2–3 minutes. Season with salt.

Return the chicken to the casserole dish and add sufficient water just to cover. Bring to the boil, cover with a lid and transfer to the preheated oven. Cook for about 1 hour.

Return the casserole dish to the stovetop and uncover. Using a slotted spoon, transfer the chicken and vegetables to a large serving platter. Cook the juices over medium heat for 3–5 minutes to reduce slightly, then stir in the cream. Bring to the boil, then reduce the heat and simmer gently, uncovered, for 5 minutes. Stir in the mustard, parsley and chives and a few grinds of black pepper. Taste for seasoning and adjust as necessary. Pour the sauce over the chicken and vegetables and serve immediately.

roast duck à l'alsacienne with sauerkraut and frankfurters

Duck is a rich meat and sauerkraut make a perfect complement, both in flavour and goodness. Served with frankfurters and bacon, this hearty recipe is one of the traditional dishes of Alsace. It can be served with potatoes (roasted in duck fat if you have any).

1 jar sauerkraut, about 800 g/1 lb. 12 oz.

250 g/9 oz. streaky bacon or smoked pork hock, cut into chunks or slices

12 frankfurters

1 duck, about 3 kg/6 lbs. 8 oz.

sea salt and freshly ground black pepper

an instant-read thermometer

Serves 6

Empty the sauerkraut into a saucepan. Cover with boiling water and bring to the boil again. Drain, discarding the water (unless you like very strong sauerkraut) and top up again with more water, then bring to the boil. Add the pieces of bacon or hock and simmer for 80 minutes. When the sauerkraut is tender, drain off this water into another saucepan, add the frankfurters and reheat just before serving (they are already cooked). Put the sauerkraut aside.

Meanwhile, sprinkle the duck with salt and pepper and put in a roasting pan without any oil. Roast in a preheated oven at 200°C (400°F) Gas 6 for 1½ hours, first on one side for 30 minutes, then the other for 20 minutes and finally on its back, or until an instant-read thermometer registers 82°C (180°F) at the thickest part of the thigh.

Remove the duck from the oven and let rest for 10 minutes. Remove the bird from the roasting pan, draining any juices from the cavity back into the pan. Put the duck on a carving board, pull back the legs and cut off at the joints. Cut each one into thigh and drumstick. Slice off the breasts and cut each one in half. Put on a heatproof plate and keep them warm. Reserve the carcass to make a stock for another occasion.

Spoon off all but about 2 tablespoons of the fat from the roasting pan into a heatproof container and keep for another occasion. Add the drained sauerkraut to the fat in the pan and mix well. Pile it all onto a large serving dish, add the heated frankfurters and the pieces of duck with its juices, then serve.

braised duck and white bean cassoulet

The idea of long-simmered duck in a garlicky sauce is always appetizing, but not always easy to achieve due to time constraints. This is shortcut cassoulet, but cassoulet in spirit because it combines duck with smoked bacon and a browned topping of white beans. It's a good dish for cold weather and easy to prepare in advance.

4 duck legs (about 400 g/14 oz. each)

2 onions, halved and sliced

1 large carrot, diced

150 g/5 oz. pancetta or lardons, diced

1 teaspoon dried thyme

4 garlic cloves, sliced

250 ml/1 cup dry white wine

2 x 400-g/14-oz. cans chopped tomatoes

125 g/1 cup pitted green olives

1 bay leaf

2 x 400-g/14-oz. cans haricot or cannellini beans, drained

about 100 g/1 cup breadcrumbs

sea salt and freshly ground black pepper

a 33 x 21-cm/13 x 9-inch baking dish

Serves 4–6

Preheat the oven to 170°C (325°F) Gas 3.

Arrange the duck legs skin-side down in a large saucepan and cook over medium heat for 4–5 minutes on each side, until browned. Transfer to a plate, sprinkle with salt.

Drain off all but 1 tablespoon of fat from the pan. Add the onions and carrots and cook for about 5 minutes, until soft. Add the pancetta and thyme and cook for a further 3–4 minutes. Add the garlic and cook for 1 minute. Season and add the wine. Bring to the boil and cook, uncovered, for 1 minute. Add the tomatoes, olives and bay leaf. Reduce the heat and simmer, uncovered, for 5 minutes. Taste and adjust the seasoning if necessary.

Using tongs, transfer the duck legs to the baking dish. Pour over the sauce and spread evenly. If necessary, add sufficient water to submerge the duck by about 2.5 cm/1 inch. Cover tightly with foil and transfer to the preheated oven to cook for 1½ hours. Check after 1 hour. (The recipe can be prepared up to 24 hours in advance up to this point. Cover and refrigerate until needed.)

Remove the baking dish from the oven and increase the heat to 200°C (400°F) Gas 6.

Add the beans to the dish in an even layer, sprinkle the breadcrumbs over the top and season well. Return to the oven and bake for 20–25 minutes more, until well browned on top. Serve immediately.

Asian beef braise with pak-choi

2 tablespoons vegetable oil

1 kg/1¼ lbs. braising steak, cut into bite-sized pieces

1 garlic clove, crushed

1 large shallot, sliced

2.5-cm/1-inch piece of fresh ginger, peeled and grated

750 ml/3 cups beef stock

125 ml/½ cup Chinese rice wine

125 ml/½ cup hoisin sauce

¼ teaspoon ground cumin

1 star anise

1 fresh red chilli/chile, sliced

freshly squeezed juice of 1 tangerine (or ½ an orange)

1 teaspoon clear honey

4–6 pak-choi

your choice of noodles, to serve

Serves 4

Heat the oil in a large saucepan. Add the steak and cook until browned. Transfer to a plate, season and set aside.

Add the garlic, shallot and ginger to the saucepan and cook, stirring constantly for 1 minute. Add the stock, rice wine, hoisin sauce, cumin, star anise, chilli/chile, tangerine juice and honey. Stir to blend and bring to the boil. Return the steak to the saucepan, reduce the heat and simmer very gently, uncovered, for 1–1½ hours, until the meat is tender. Taste and adjust the seasoning.

Core the pak-choi. Cut the white part into 1-cm/½-inch slices; leave the greens large or cut in half. Add the white part to the saucepan, increase the heat and cook for 3–4 minutes until just tender. Add the greens and cook until just wilted, about 2–3 minutes more. Serve immediately with cooked noodles of your choice.

ginger and star anise braised chicken

1 tablespoon vegetable oil

1 medium chicken (800–900 g/2 lbs.), cut into serving pieces

2.5-cm/1-inch piece of fresh ginger, peeled and cut into thin strips

3 garlic cloves, sliced

80 ml/⅓ cup Chinese rice wine

125 ml/½ cup chicken stock or water

1 tablespoon clear honey

1 star anise

60 ml/¼ cup light soy sauce

freshly squeezed juice of 1 clementine (or 3–4 tablespoons fresh orange juice)

2 spring onions/scallions, thinly sliced

rice, to serve

sea salt

Serves 4

Heat the oil in a large saucepan. When hot, add the chicken pieces, skin-side down, and cook for about 4–5 minutes on each side, until browned. Transfer to a plate, season lightly with salt and set aside.

Drain all but 1 tablespoon of fat from the pan. Add the ginger, garlic, rice wine, stock, honey, star anise and soy sauce and bring to the boil. Add the clementine juice and the chicken. Reduce the heat, cover and simmer gently for 15 minutes. Turn the chicken pieces and simmer for about 15 minutes more, until cooked through. Taste and adjust the seasoning if necessary.

Remove the chicken from the pan with a slotted spoon and set aside. Bring the liquid back to the boil and cook for 2–3 minutes to reduce slightly. Remove the star anise, return the chicken to the pan and stir to coat in the sauce. Sprinkle with spring onions/scallions and serve with rice.

Hungarian goulash

1 tablespoon vegetable oil

2 onions, diced

1 red bell pepper, diced

1 green bell pepper, diced

1 teaspoon caraway seeds

2 generous teaspoons paprika, sweet or hot, or half and half

750 g/1½ lbs. stewing beef, cut into small cubes

3 large ripe tomatoes, peeled, cored, deseeded and chopped

1 tablespoon tomato purée/paste

3 carrots, diced

375 ml/1½ cups beef stock

2 bay leaves

400-g/14-oz. can kidney beans, drained

a large handful of fresh parsley leaves, chopped

sea salt and freshly ground black pepper

wide egg noodles or ribbon pasta, to serve

Serves 4

Heat the oil in a large saucepan. Add the onions and peppers and cook until soft. Season with a little salt and add the caraway seeds and paprika. Cook for 1 minute. Add the cubed beef. Cook, stirring occasionally, for 2–3 minutes, until browned. Season with a little more salt if liked.

Add the tomatoes, tomato purée/paste, carrots, stock and bay leaves, and season lightly. Simmer, uncovered, for at least 40 minutes. Add the kidney beans and cook for 10 minutes more (do not be tempted to add the beans any earlier as they will become tough if overcooked).

Sprinkle with the parsley and serve spooned over egg noodles or ribbon pasta.

spiced lamb tagine with prunes

Tagines may sound exotic, but they couldn't be easier to prepare. This recipe is a perfect example. It is simple and satisfying, perfect as a weeknight supper but equally suited for entertaining. Serve with a watercress salad and plenty of buttery couscous.

2 onions

2 tablespoons olive oil

1 teaspoon ground turmeric

1 teaspoon ground ginger

½ teaspoon freshly ground black pepper

a pinch of saffron threads

1 teaspoon ground cumin

½ teaspoon ground cinnamon

1 kg/2¼ lbs. stewing lamb, cut into bite-sized pieces

a small bunch of fresh coriander/cilantro, firmly tied into a bundle with string

225 g/1 cup pitted soft prunes

2 tablespoons clear honey

sea salt and freshly ground black pepper

couscous, to serve

Serves 4

Finely chop 1 of the onions either by grating it on the coarse side of a grater or processing in a food processor. Put it in a large saucepan or heatproof casserole dish.

Add the oil, spices and lamb. Cook over low heat for 2–3 minutes, stirring to coat the lamb in oil, until the mixture becomes aromatic. Season well with salt. Pour in sufficient water just to cover and add the coriander/cilantro bundle. Reduce the heat, cover and simmer gently for 1½ hours.

Halve the remaining onion and slice into thin half moon slices. When the lamb is tender, remove with a slotted spoon and transfer to a dish. Cover and keep warm.

Add the sliced onion, prunes and honey to the liquid in the saucepan. Cover and cook for about 15 minutes, until the onion is tender. Remove the lid and simmer for about 5–8 minutes to reduce the sauce slightly. Return the lamb to the pan and toss well. Serve spooned over couscous.

Moroccan fish tagine

This recipe uses an ordinary baking dish, with foil in place of the conical tagine lid. Not authentic, but an acceptable replacement. Another slight modification is the use of fillets because it is more traditional to use whole fish, such as sea bass. But the herbs and spices are based on a traditional Moroccan recipe and the taste is fabulously genuine. Serve with couscous or rice, as preferred.

1 kg/1¼ lbs. boneless, skinless fish fillets

1 onion, coarsely chopped

a handful of fresh parsley leaves

2 garlic cloves, crushed

400-g/14-oz. can chopped tomatoes

4 thin carrots, halved and sliced

1 teaspoon ground cumin

½ teaspoon cayenne pepper

a pinch of sugar

sea salt and freshly ground black pepper

lemon wedges, to serve

couscous or rice, to serve

For the marinade

2 tablespoons chopped fresh coriander/cilantro leaves

1 tablespoon coarse sea salt

4 garlic cloves, crushed

2 tablespoons paprika

½ teaspoon cayenne pepper

1 tablespoon ground cumin

freshly squeezed juice of ½ a lemon

125 ml/½ cup olive oil

a baking dish, large enough to take the fish in a single layer

Serves 4

Combine the coriander/cilantro, salt, garlic, paprika, cayenne, cumin, lemon juice and olive oil in a shallow baking dish (not metal) large enough to hold the fish in a single layer. Mix well. Add the fish, and use your hands to turn the pieces until they are coated in the oil. Cover with clingfilm/plastic wrap and refrigerate while you prepare the sauce (at least 30 minutes and up to several hours).

Preheat the oven to 190°C (375°F) Gas 5.

To make the sauce, put the onion, parsley and garlic in a food processor and process until finely chopped. Transfer to a saucepan set over medium heat. Add the tomatoes, 300 ml/1¼ cups water, carrots, cumin, cayenne and sugar. Season and stir to blend. Bring to the boil, then reduce the heat and simmer, covered, for about 15 minutes, until the carrots are tender.

Remove the fish from the refrigerator. Transfer it to a plate and pour the tomato sauce into the baking dish containing the marinade and mix well. Return the fish to the dish, arranging it on top of the sauce. Cover with foil and bake in the preheated oven for 10–20 minutes, until the fish is cooked through.

Remove from the oven, sprinkle with the coriander/cilantro sprigs and grind over some black pepper. Serve with the lemon wedges on the side for squeezing and couscous or rice, as preferred.

coconut chicken curry with spiced lentil dhal and potatoes

This is a long list of ingredients, but the dish comes together very quickly so don't let it put you off. As with most highly spiced dishes, this benefits from being made in advance, to allow the spices time to mingle. Serve with rice and warmed naan bread.

3 tablespoons vegetable oil

450 g/1 lb. boneless chicken, cut into pieces

3 tablespoons garam masala

200 ml/¾ cup coconut milk

3 tablespoons cumin seeds

2 tablespoons black mustard seeds

1 onion, very finely chopped

2.5-cm/1½-inch piece of fresh ginger, peeled and grated

3 garlic cloves, crushed

1 fresh red chilli/chile, chopped

3 teaspoons ground cumin

1 teaspoon ground turmeric

¼–1 teaspoon cayenne pepper, to taste

1 tablespoon tomato purée/paste

500 ml/2 cups chicken stock

1 cinnamon stick

250 g/1¼ cups split red lentils

350 g/12 oz. new potatoes, scrubbed or peeled and cubed

150 g/1 cup frozen peas

1 tablespoon clear honey

freshly squeezed juice of 1 lemon

sea salt

a handful of fresh coriander/cilantro leaves, to serve

rice and/or warmed naan bread, to serve

Serves 6–8

Heat 1 tablespoon of the oil in a large frying pan set over medium heat. Add the chicken and 2 tablespoons of the garam masala and season well with salt. Cook for 3–5 minutes, stirring, until golden. Add the coconut milk and simmer for about 10 minutes, until the chicken is cooked. Set aside.

Heat the remaining oil in a large saucepan. Add the cumin and mustard seeds and cook until they begin to sputter. Stir in the onion, ginger, garlic, chilli/chile, cumin, turmeric, cayenne, tomato purée/paste and remaining garam masala and cook, stirring, for 1–2 minutes.

Add the stock, 200 ml/¾ cup water, cinnamon, lentils and potatoes and mix well. Reduce the heat and simmer, uncovered, for 35–45 minutes, until the potatoes are tender. Check often and top up with water if required; the mixture should be liquid but not overly soupy. Taste and adjust the seasoning if necessary. Stir in the honey and lemon juice.

Stir the chicken mixture into the lentil mixture. Add the peas and simmer for 5 minutes more. Sprinkle with coriander/cilantro and serve with rice and naan bread.

Variation: For a vegetarian version, replace the chicken with 500 g/1 lb. cauliflower florets, and simmer in the coconut milk until tender, before adding to the lentils.

Thai red beef curry

This is a truly straightforward curry recipe. There are many brands of curry paste available, some better than others, but if you find a good one, this will taste remarkably authentic. In reality, you could simply stop at the curry paste and coconut milk, but adding more lemongrass and ginger makes this dish even more flavoursome. And, the fish sauce and palm sugar give the finished dish more depth. Use this as a blueprint recipe for any Thai red curry and experiment with different ingredients in place of the beef. Boneless chicken or prawns/shrimp work well, as do a mixture of vegetables such as baby corn, aubergine/eggplant, sweet potato and broccoli. Serve with basmati rice, either steamed or boiled.

1 tablespoon vegetable oil

800 g/1½ lbs. sirloin steak, sliced into thin strips

4 tablespoons Thai red curry paste

2 x 400-g/14-oz. cans coconut milk

½ lemongrass stalk, white part only, very finely chopped

1–2 tablespoons Thai fish sauce, to taste

2.5-cm/1-inch piece of fresh ginger, peeled and grated

1 tablespoon palm sugar or clear honey

300 g/10 oz. green beans, cut into 2.5-cm/1-inch lengths

steamed basmati rice, to serve

Serves 4

Heat the oil in a large saucepan. Add the beef and cook for 2–3 minutes, stirring, until just browned. Add the curry paste and continue cooking for 1–2 minutes, stirring occasionally to coat the meat.

Add the coconut milk, lemongrass, 1 tablespoon of the fish sauce, ginger and sugar. Stir well, reduce the heat, and simmer gently for 15 minutes. Taste and add the remaining tablespoon of fish sauce if necessary. Continue simmering, uncovered, for about 15 minutes more.

Add the green beans, part cover and simmer gently for about 10 minutes more until the beans are just tender. Serve immediately with plenty of rice.

There's nothing like a spicy, aromatic curry or tagine to warm you up on a cold day – perfect for sharing with family and friends.

seafood and yellow split pea curry

The Thai Red Beef Curry recipe (page 89) uses a ready-made curry paste, but a basic curry paste is easy to make from a few storecupboard spices and a handful of fresh seasonings. The split peas used here cook down to a mushy consistency, thickening the sauce nicely.

1 large onion, roughly chopped

3 garlic cloves, chopped

5-cm/2-inch piece of fresh ginger, peeled and chopped

2 large fresh red chillies/chiles, chopped

1 tablespoon vegetable oil

500 g/1 lb. 2 oz. raw king prawns/shrimp, peeled and deveined

6–8 curry leaves (dried or fresh)

½ teaspoon ground cumin

½ teaspoon turmeric

4 ripe tomatoes, roughly chopped

55 g/¼ cup dried yellow split peas

leaves from a small bunch of fresh coriander/cilantro, roughly chopped

sea salt and freshly ground black pepper

cooked basmati rice, to serve

Serves 4

Put the onion, garlic, ginger and chillies/chiles in a food processor and process to a paste.

Heat the oil in a large frying pan set over high heat. Add the prawns/shrimp and cook for just 2 minutes on each side, until pink. Remove from the pan and set aside.

Add the onion mixture to the pan and stir-fry for 5 minutes, until starting to turn golden. Add the curry leaves and cook for 1 minute. Stir in the cumin and turmeric and cook for 1 minute more, until aromatic.

Add the tomatoes, 125 ml/½ cup cold water and the split peas. Let the mixture sizzle and boil for 1 minute, then reduce the heat to a low simmer. Cook for 25–30 minutes, until the split peas are just tender and the mixture has thickened. Return the cooked prawns/shrimp to the pan and add the coriander/cilantro. Cook for 2 minutes, until the prawns/shrimp are heated through. Season well with salt and pepper and serve with basmati rice.

Vegetarian option: Dice about 400 g/14 oz. paneer (Indian cheese) and fry in a non-stick frying pan set over medium heat. Substitute for the prawns, following the recipe as above.

sweet potato, spinach and chickpea stew with coconut

This falls somewhere between a stew and a soup and is delicious served with fragrant jasmine rice to soak up the abundant sauce. If you like things spicy, add two chillies/chiles and all their seeds; if not, add one but discard the seeds. It will be very mild and the specks of red are pretty against the orange.

1 tablespoon vegetable oil

1 onion, halved and sliced

5-cm/2-inch piece of fresh ginger, peeled and grated

1–2 fresh red chillies/chiles, halved and sliced

1 teaspoon curry powder

1 teaspoon ground cumin

1.3 kg/3 lbs. sweet potatoes, peeled and cubed

400-ml/14-oz. can coconut milk

450 ml/1¾ cups vegetable stock

1 tablespoon Thai fish sauce (optional)

400-g/14-oz. can chickpeas, drained

225 g/8 oz. fresh baby spinach leaves, washed

sea salt

jasmine rice, to serve

Serves 4–6

Heat the oil in a large saucepan. Add the onion and cook over low heat for 3–5 minutes, until just soft. Add the ginger, chillies/chiles, curry powder, cumin and a pinch of salt. Cook for 1–2 minutes, stirring, until aromatic.

Add the sweet potatoes and stir to coat in the spices. Add the coconut milk and stock and a little water if necessary, just to cover the sweet potatoes; the mixture should be soupy as it will cook down. Add the fish sauce (if using) or some salt, if preferred. Bring to the boil, then simmer, uncovered, for 15 minutes.

Add the chickpeas and continue to simmer for 15–20 minutes more, until the sweet potatoes are tender.

Add the spinach, in batches, stirring to blend and waiting for each batch to wilt before adding the next. Taste and adjust the seasoning if necessary. Serve immediately with jasmine rice.

When it's freezing outside, where better to be than at the heart of a warm kitchen enjoying the aromas of good home cooking wafting from the oven.

slow-cooked pork belly with beans and miso

This hearty and nutritious dish is packed full of all the goodness of soya/soy beans. They are, however, quite bland and need plenty of robust ingredients with distinctive flavours cooking alongside them. The Asian flavours here do the job nicely making a satisfying and flavoursome dish.

100 g/⅔ cup dried soya/soy beans
1 kg/2 lbs. 4 oz. pork belly, in 1 piece
125 ml/½ cup sake (Japanese rice wine)
1 tablespoon peanut oil
2 teaspoons sesame oil
3 garlic cloves, roughly chopped
4 spring onions/scallions, white parts only, chopped
5 thin slices fresh ginger
250 ml/1 cup chicken or vegetable stock
2 tablespoons light soy sauce
2 tablespoons white miso (soya/soy bean paste)
1 teaspoon sugar
½ teaspoon sea salt

a large, heatproof casserole dish

Serves 4

Soak the beans in 750 ml/3 cups cold water for at least 10 hours or overnight. Drain and transfer to a large saucepan.

Add plenty of boiling water and set the pan over medium heat. Cook for 45–50 minutes, until the beans are tender. Drain and set aside.

Cut the pork belly into 8 pieces. Put them in a dish and pour over the sake. Cover with clingfilm/plastic wrap and set aside for 1 hour, turning often. Remove the pork from the sake, reserving the sake.

Put the peanut oil in a heatproof casserole dish and set over high heat. Cook the pork in batches (so as not to overcrowd the pan), for 4–5 minutes, turning until golden all over. Put the browned pork in a bowl and set aside.

Preheat the oven to 160°C (325°F) Gas 3.

Add the sesame oil to the casserole dish. Add the garlic, spring onions/scallions and ginger and stir-fry for 1–2 minutes, until aromatic and softened. Add the reserved sake, letting it boil, and cook until the liquid has reduced by half, stirring to remove any stuck-on bits of pork from the bottom of the casserole dish. Add the stock, soy sauce, miso, sugar and salt and return the pork to the pan, stirring until the miso dissolves. Bring to the boil, cover with a tight-fitting lid, transfer to the preheated oven and cook for 2 hours, turning the pork after 1 hour. Stir in the soya beans, cover and cook for 30 minutes more. Serve hot.

slow-cooked lamb shanks with lentils

This recipe is so delicious – if you make it once, you may be hooked. For a lighter version, try chicken instead of lamb; choose some lovely Maryland cuts (thigh and drumstick), pan-sear until the skin is golden, then proceed with the recipe from there. Serve this with creamy mashed potatoes and green beans.

100 g/⅔ cup dried green lentils
100 g/3½ oz. pancetta or streaky bacon, chopped
2 garlic cloves, chopped
400-g/14-oz. can chopped tomatoes
500 ml/2 cups chicken stock
250 ml/1 cup red wine
4 trimmed lamb shanks
a handful of fresh flat-leaf parsley leaves, roughly chopped
sea salt and freshly ground black pepper

a large casserole dish or other lidded baking dish

Serves 4

Preheat the oven to 160°C (325°F) Gas 3.

Put the lentils, pancetta, garlic, tomatoes, stock and wine in a large casserole dish and season well with salt and pepper. Stir well to combine. Add the lamb shanks and cover with a tight-fitting lid.

Cook in the preheated oven for 1½ hours. Remove the casserole dish from the oven and turn the lamb shanks over. Re-cover, return to the oven and cook for 1 hour more, until the lamb is tender. Stir in the parsley. Serve one shank per person with a generous portion of the lentils.

slow-roasted pork loin with rosemary, madeira and orange

1.5 kg/3 lb. centre loin of pork
200 ml/¾ cup Madeira wine
100 ml/⅓ cup freshly squeezed orange juice
2 sprigs of rosemary, bruised
2 oranges, peeled and sliced into 4 slices each

sea salt and freshly ground black pepper

thick kitchen foil
an instant-read thermometer

Serves 4

Score the fat with a criss cross pattern and season the meat with plenty of salt and pepper, rubbing it in well. Put a double thickness of kitchen foil in a large roasting pan and turn up the edges. Put in the meat fat side down and pour in the Madeira and juice. Add the rosemary. Leave for about 2 hours if possible, then put in the middle of a preheated oven at 170°C (325°F) Gas 3 and slow-roast for 1 hour.

Carefully turn the meat over, then add the orange slices and about 125 ml/½ cup water if it is starting to dry out. Cook for a further 30 minutes. Then raise the oven temperature to 220°C (425°F) Gas 7 for a final 10 minutes or until an instant-read thermometer registers 80°C (175°F).

Lift the meat onto a serving dish and arrange the orange slices around it. Pour the juices into a gravy boat and serve.

mustard and herb chicken baked in a salt crust

1 chicken, 1.5–1.8 kg/ 3 lbs. 5 oz.–4 lbs.
1 lemon, cut in half
3 tablespoons Dijon mustard
1 tablespoon herbes de Provence

5 egg whites
1.8 kg/4 lbs. coarse sea salt
cracked black pepper

a roasting pan or baking dish

Serves 6

Preheat the oven to 190°C (375°F) Gas 5.

Stuff the chicken with the lemon halves and rub the mustard all over the skin. Sprinkle with the herbes de Provence and season with cracked black pepper. Set the chicken aside.

In a large bowl lightly beat the egg whites until frothy. Add the salt and mix thoroughly. The mixture should be the consistency of wet sand.

Spread a thin layer of salt evenly on the bottom of the roasting pan or baking dish. Put the chicken on top and cover with the rest of the salt mixture. Pat down and make sure there are no holes from which the steam can escape.

Bake the chicken in the preheated oven for 1 hour. You'll notice that the salt will turn a golden brown. Remove the chicken from the oven and leave it to rest for 10 minutes.

spiced roast ham or pork with juniper berries

This dish is for Christmas time – the spices lightly pickle the meat and give it an intriguing Eastern flavour. They must be rubbed in dry so the flavours penetrate the meat, then later the oil is added to moisten it. Because there is a great deal of fatless meat on a ham, it will dry out and toughen unless basted frequently. If you are using the trotter end of a half leg, wrap it with a thick collar of kitchen foil during the later part of the cooking to keep it moist. The meat taken from the top end of the leg may be tunnel-boned for easier carving. It is delicious cold.

½ leg of pork or gammon, about 2.5 kg/5½ lbs.
2–3 tablespoons peanut or sunflower oil
275 ml/1¼ cups water or chicken stock
sea salt

Spice mixture
1 teaspoon ground coriander
1 teaspoon ground cumin
1 teaspoon ground caraway
1 teaspoon ground ginger
½ teaspoon ground cinnamon
½ teaspoon ground allspice
½ teaspoon freshly grated nutmeg
12 juniper berries, crushed

an instant-read thermometer

Serves 6

To prepare the spice mixture, put the ground coriander, cumin, caraway, ginger, cinnamon, allspice, nutmeg and juniper berries in a bowl and mix well. Remove the rind from the meat and rub the dry spices into all the crevices in the meat. Wrap it in clingfilm/plastic wrap or a plastic bag and refrigerate for 48 hours.

Score the fat with a criss cross pattern on the upper side of the meat. Put in a roasting pan, baste with the oil and season well with salt. Put the pan in the middle of a preheated oven at 240°C (475°F) Gas 8 and add 5–6 tablespoons water. Roast for 10 minutes, then reduce the temperature to 170°C (325°F) Gas 3 and cook for 2½ hours. Baste from time to time and add extra water as necessary to keep it moist because this will form the base of the gravy.

When an instant-read thermometer reaches 80°C (175°F), transfer the meat to a serving dish and let it rest for 10 minutes.

Meanwhile, deglaze the pan with the water or stock to make a gravy, then boil to reduce and intensify the flavours. Taste and, if necessary, adjust the seasoning. Carve the meat in slices and serve the gravy separately in a gravy boat.

rolled roast pork with sage and onion stuffing

2 kg/4 lbs. blade or hand of pork/pork arm roast or Boston butt, with rind if possible, and scored

1 teaspoon sea salt

2 tablespoons olive oil, for brushing

Stuffing

1 onion, finely chopped

1 green apple, such as Granny Smith, cut into small pieces

2 celery stalks, finely chopped

60 g/½ cup chopped cashew nuts

50 g/4 tablespoons unsalted butter

2 teaspoons chopped fresh sage leaves

grated zest and freshly squeezed juice of 1 unwaxed lemon

250 g/5 cups fresh breadcrumbs

Cider gravy

125 ml/½ cup cider vinegar

250 ml/1 cup water or chicken stock

a roasting pan with a rack

a baking sheet with sides, or Swiss roll/jelly roll pan

an instant-read thermometer

Serves 6

To make the stuffing, put the onion, apple, celery, cashews, butter, sage, lemon zest and juice and breadcrumbs in a bowl. Mix well.

Season the inside of the pork with the salt, then spread the stuffing over that side, roll up the meat and tie it with string to make a good shape. Brush with the oil and set it on a rack in a roasting pan. Add 250 ml/1 cup water. Put it in a cold oven, turn the heat to 220°C (425°F) Gas 7 and roast for 30 minutes.

Reduce the oven temperature to 170°C (325°F) Gas 3. Cook for another 1½ hours or until an instant-read thermometer registers 80°C (175°F). Transfer the meat to another roasting pan or a baking sheet with sides. Do not baste during this time.

Raise the oven temperature to maximum and return the meat to the very hot oven for another 20 minutes to crisp the surface.

Meanwhile, make the gravy by deglazing the roasting pan with the vinegar and reducing it well. Add the water or stock, bring to the boil, then taste and adjust the seasoning with salt if necessary. Serve in a gravy boat.

When the meat is ready, transfer the roast to a carving platter and let rest for 10–20 minutes before carving into fairly thick slices.

jasmine-brined roasted poussins with salsa verde

2 poussins weighing 700 g/1 lb. 9 oz. (or 1 Cornish game hen)

1 small unwaxed lemon

1 garlic clove, crushed

1 tablespoon olive oil

sea salt and cracked black pepper

Brining solution

4 tablespoons jasmine tea or 4 jasmine teabags

1.5 litres/6 cups boiling water

60 g/2¼ oz. coarse rock salt

1 tablespoon dark brown soft sugar

Salsa verde

20 g/½ cup flat-leaf parsley leaves

20 g/½ cup coriander/cilantro leaves

20 g/½ cup mint leaves

2 garlic cloves, finely chopped

finely grated zest of 1 small unwaxed lemon

1 tablespoon brined capers

125 ml/½ cup olive oil

a roasting pan, kitchen string

Serves 2

First make the brine. Put the jasmine tea in a large measuring jug/pitcher and pour over the boiling water. Add the salt and sugar and stir until dissolved. Set aside to cool completely.

Wash and dry the poussins and put in a deep dish. Pour the cooled brine over them, cover, and refrigerate for 6–8 hours.

When you are ready to cook, preheat the oven to 190°C (375°F) Gas 5. Remove the poussins from the brining mixture and pat dry, removing any leftover tea leaves. Discard the brining mixture; it cannot be used again.

Put the poussins in a roasting pan. Zest the lemon and reserve for the Salsa Verde. Cut the lemon into quarters and stuff the cavity with them. Tie the legs together with kitchen string. Mix together the garlic and oil and rub over the skin of the poussins. Season with salt and pepper.

Roast in the preheated oven for 35 minutes until cooked and the poussin juices run clear.

To make the Salsa Verde, put all the salsa ingredients in a food processor and pulse until roughly chopped. Be careful not to overprocess; you want the salsa to be slightly chunky. Season with sea salt and black pepper.

When the poussins are ready, remove from the oven and set aside to rest for 10 minutes, covered with kitchen foil, in a warm place. Carve and serve with the Salsa Verde.

root vegetable gratin

3 small turnips (about 375 g/13 oz.), halved and thinly sliced

½ a celeriac (about 325 g/ 11 oz.), halved and thinly sliced

½ a swede (about 450 g/1 lb.), halved and thinly sliced

650 g/1½ lbs. waxy potatoes, halved and thinly sliced

225 ml/scant 1 cup double/heavy cream

100 g/6 tablespoons crème fraîche/sour cream

250 ml/1 cup milk

125 g/1 cup grated Gruyère or medium Cheddar

sea salt and freshly ground black pepper

a 30 x 20-cm/12 x 8-inch baking dish, greased

Serves 4–6

Preheat the oven to 200°C (400°F) Gas 6.

Put all the vegetable slices in a large bowl and mix to combine. Set aside.

Combine the cream, crème fraîche/sour cream and milk in a small saucepan and heat just to melt the crème fraîche/sour cream. Stir well, season with salt and pepper.

Arrange half of the vegetables slices in the prepared baking dish. Sprinkle with a little salt and one-third of the cheese. Pour over one-third of the cream mixture. Top with the rest of the vegetable slices, the remaining cheese and a sprinkle of salt. Pour over the remaining cream mixture and bake in the preheated oven for 1–1½ hours, until browned on top. Serve immediately.

winter vegetable bake

280 g/10 oz. Brussels sprouts, trimmed and quartered

2–3 tablespoons olive oil

500 g/1 lb. cauliflower florets

750 g/1½ lbs. waxy potatoes

200 ml/¾ cup crème fraîche/sour cream

125 ml/½ cup single/light cream

50 g/½ cup fresh breadcrumbs

a pinch of paprika

1 onion, halved and thinly sliced

125 g/1½ cups grated mature/sharp Cheddar

2–3 tablespoons freshly grated Parmesan

sea salt and freshly ground black pepper

a 30 x 20-cm/12 x 8-inch baking dish, greased

Serves 4–6

Preheat the oven to 200°C (400°F) Gas 6.

Toss the Brussels sprouts with the oil until coated, season with salt and spread out in a single layer on a baking sheet. Roast in the preheated oven for 25–30 minutes, until just tender.

Meanwhile, bring a large saucepan of water to the boil. Add the cauliflower florets and a pinch of salt and blanch for 5–8 minutes, until just tender. Drain. When cool enough to handle, slice thinly and set aside. Bring another large saucepan of salted water to the boil, add the potatoes and cook until just tender when pierced with a knife. Drain. When cool enough to handle, slice the potatoes thinly and set aside.

In a bowl, whisk together the crème fraîche/sour cream and cream and season well. The mixture should be thick, but thin enough to pour – add a spoonful of milk to thin if required. Set aside. Season the breadcrumbs and stir in the paprika. Set aside.

Arrange the potato slices in the prepared baking dish and lay the onion slices on top. Sprinkle with salt and half of the cheese. Arrange the cauliflower slices on top of the cheese, then sprinkle with the remaining cheese. Pour over the cream mixture. Top with the roasted Brussels sprouts in an even layer. Cover with foil and bake in the preheated oven for 30 minutes. After 30 minutes, remove from the oven. Remove the foil, sprinkle with the breadcrumbs and Parmesan and bake for a further 30–40 minutes, until browned. Serve immediately.

butternut squash, corn and bread bake with cheese and chives

1 tablespoon olive oil

1 large onion, halved and thinly sliced

375 ml/1½ cups milk

225 ml/scant 1 cup single/light cream

3 eggs, beaten

a small bunch of chives, snipped

leaves from a small bunch of fresh parsley, finely chopped

1 baguette, neatly cut into ½-cm/⅛-inch slices

300 g/2 cups (sweet) corn kernels, canned or frozen

about 500 g/1 lb 2 oz. peeled and sliced butternut squash

100 g/1 cup grated mature/sharp Cheddar

sea salt and freshly ground black pepper

a 30 x 20-cm/12 x 8-inch baking dish, greased

Serves 4–6

Preheat the oven to 190°C (375°F) Gas 5.

Heat the oil in a large frying pan. Add the onion and cook over low heat for 3–5 minutes, until soft. Season lightly and set aside.

Combine the milk, cream and eggs in a small bowl and whisk to combine. Season with 1½ teaspoons salt. Add the chives and parsley, mix well and set aside.

Arrange half the baguette slices in the prepared baking dish in a single layer; you may need to tear some to cover all the space. Put half of the onion slices on top, then scatter over half of the corn. Arrange half of the squash slices evenly on top and sprinkle with half of the cheese. Repeat one more time (bread, onion, corn, squash, cheese). Stir the milk mixture and pour it evenly all over the pudding.

Cover tightly with foil and bake in the preheated oven for 20 minutes. Remove the foil and continue baking for about 30–40 minutes, until golden. Serve immediately.

winter
salads

There's nothing quite like a plate of nutritious and satisfying food to stave off those winter blues. Be good to yourself and prepare some nourishing winter salads. You'll be surprised how many delicious variations you can create using simple ingredients.

cheese, apple and hazelnut autumn salad

A pretty autumnal salad that is substantial enough to serve as a main meal.

25 g/¼ cup shelled hazelnuts
1 tablespoon sunflower oil
100 g/3½ oz. smoked bacon lardons or pancetta cubes
1 Little Gem lettuce, leaves separated
75 g/2½ oz. smoked chicken, torn into strips
60 g/2¼ oz. Comté or Beaufort (rind removed), thinly sliced on the diagonal
1 Cox or Blenheim Orange apple, quartered, cored and cut into wedges
a few root vegetable crisps/chips
a small handful of fresh chives, snipped

Dressing
2 tablespoons crab apple jelly, rowan jelly or redcurrant jelly
2 tablespoons pure apple juice
1 teaspoon cider vinegar
sea salt and freshly ground black pepper

Serves 2

Preheat the oven to 180°C (350°F) Gas 4.

Put the hazelnuts on a baking sheet and roast in the preheated oven for 10 minutes until the skins turn dark brown. Leave to cool, then tip them onto a clean dish towel and rub off the skins. Cut the hazelnuts in half.

Heat the oil in a frying pan and fry the bacon until crisp. Take the pan off the heat, remove the bacon from the pan with a slotted spoon and transfer to a plate lined with paper towels. Pour off all but 1 tablespoon of the fat, add the crab apple jelly for the dressing and stir until melted, putting the pan back on the heat if necessary. Add the apple juice and cider vinegar and a splash of water if needed to thin the dressing. Season with salt and pepper and set aside.

Take 2 plates and arrange the lettuce leaves on each plate. Top with the bacon and smoked chicken, then the cheese and apple. Drizzle over the dressing and scatter with the hazelnuts, a few root vegetable crisps/chips and the chives. Serve immediately with the remaining root vegetable crisps/chips in a bowl on the side.

apple, beetroot and fennel salad with roquefort

This is a colourful combination of crisp ingredients that will liven up any meal. The mix of flavours and textures is very pleasing; if fennel is unavailable, you could substitute thinly sliced celery.

1 bunch of watercress, stems trimmed, leaves rinsed and dried
2 red or green apples, such as Gala or Granny Smith, halved, cored and thinly sliced
1 fennel bulb, halved and thinly sliced
75 g/2½ oz. Roquefort cheese, crumbled
a handful of flat-leaf parsley, finely chopped
a small bunch of chives, snipped
2 cooked beetroot/beets, sliced

For the vinaigrette
2 tablespoons red or white wine vinegar
1 teaspoon fine sea salt
1 teaspoon Dijon mustard
7 tablespoons sunflower oil
1 tablespoon crème fraîche/sour cream
freshly ground black pepper

Serves 4

First, prepare the vinaigrette. Put the vinegar in a bowl. Using a fork or a small whisk, stir in the salt until almost dissolved. Stir in the mustard. Stir in the oil, a tablespoon at a time, whisking well between each addition, until emulsified. Finally, stir in the crème fraîche/sour cream and add pepper to taste.

Just before you're ready to serve the salad, tear the watercress into pieces and put it in a bowl with the apples, fennel, cheese, parsley and chives. Pour over all but 2 tablespoons of the vinaigrette and toss gently with your hands. Divide the salad between serving plates and top each portion with beetroot/beets. Drizzle the remaining vinaigrette over the top of each and serve immediately.

Winter food doesn't have to be heavy to be satisfying. Making delicious, hearty salads is the perfect way to enjoy the best ingredients the season has to offer.

pear and parmesan salad with endive and walnuts

600 g/1 lb. 5 oz. chicory/
Belgian endives (about
4–5), cored, halved and very
thinly sliced

2 ripe pears, such as Williams,
cored and thinly sliced

75–100 g/2½ –3½ oz.
Parmesan, shaved

75 g/½ cup chopped walnuts

a handful of flat-leaf parsley,
finely chopped

For the vinaigrette

2 tablespoons cider vinegar

1 teaspoon fine sea salt

1 teaspoon Dijon mustard

7 tablespoons sunflower oil

1 tablespoon walnut oil
(optional)

freshly ground black pepper

Serves 4

First, prepare the vinaigrette. Put the vinegar in a bowl.
Using a fork or a small whisk, stir in the salt until almost
dissolved. Stir in the mustard. Stir in the oil, a tablespoon
at a time, whisking well between each addition, until
emulsified. (Note: If you're using the walnut oil, use
1 less tablespoon sunflower oil.) Add pepper to taste.

Just before you're ready to serve, put the salad ingredients
in a bowl, pour over the vinaigrette and toss to combine.
Divide between serving plates and serve immediately.

roasted butternut squash with spiced lentils, goat cheese and walnuts

This recipe will fill your kitchen with appetizing and exotic aromas. You can use pumpkin or sweet potato in place of the squash, or a combination of the two, as long as the weight is roughly the same as that of a butternut squash. Serve with plenty of crusty bread.

275 g/1 cup green lentils, rinsed and drained

50 g/½ cup walnut pieces

1 butternut squash, peeled, deseeded and cubed

3 tablespoons olive oil

1 large onion, halved and sliced

1 fresh red chilli/chile, halved and sliced

1 teaspoon ground cumin

1 teaspoon ground turmeric

1 teaspoon paprika

2 garlic cloves, crushed

400-g/14-oz. can chopped tomatoes

a pinch of sugar

a large handful of fresh flat-leaf parsley leaves, chopped

a small handful of fresh coriander/cilantro leaves, finely chopped

freshly squeezed juice of ½ a lemon

250 g/9 oz. soft goat cheese or feta

sea salt and freshly ground black pepper

Serves 4

Preheat the oven to 190°C (375°F) Gas 5.

Put the lentils in a saucepan with sufficient cold water to cover. Add a pinch of salt, bring to the boil and simmer for 20–30 minutes, until tender. Drain and set aside.

Dry roast the walnuts in a small non-stick frying pan set over low heat, until browned. Set aside.

Arrange the squash cubes on a baking sheet, toss with 2 tablespoons of the oil and sprinkle with a little salt. Roast in the preheated oven for 30–35 minutes, until tender, turning halfway through cooking time.

Heat the remaining oil in a large saucepan, add the onion and cook over low heat for 3–5 minutes, until soft. Add the chilli/chile, cumin, turmeric, paprika, garlic and a pinch of salt and cook, stirring for 1 minute. Add the tomatoes, sugar, another pinch of salt, half the parsley and half the coriander/cilantro. Simmer, uncovered, for 20 minutes, stirring in the cooked lentils 5 minutes before the end of cooking time. Taste and season with salt and pepper.

Add the roasted squash, the remaining herbs and a squeeze of lemon juice. Crumble over the goat cheese, add the walnuts and serve immediately with crusty bread.

iceberg, blue cheese and date salad

Dressing

½ teaspoon saffron threads

2 tablespoons freshly squeezed orange juice

1 tablespoon white wine vinegar

½ teaspoon sea salt

6 tablespoons walnut oil

1 iceberg lettuce

200 g/1½ cups blue cheese

8 dried medjool dates

70 g/scant 1 cup walnut halves

a large handful of micro greens (sprouts)

Serves 6

To make the saffron and walnut dressing, put the saffron and orange juice in a bowl and leave to infuse for about 10 minutes. Whisk in the vinegar and salt, then the oil, whisking continuously. Cover and set aside until needed.

Slice the lettuce into 8 wedges, then cut each wedge into 3 pieces, giving you a total of 24 pieces. Arrange them in a serving bowl.

Cut the cheese into 12 pieces and arrange these among the lettuce. Chop the dates into 4 and discard the stones/pits. Scatter them over the lettuce along with the walnuts. Pour over the dressing, then scatter over the micro greens. Serve immediately.

roasted sweet potato and macadamia nut salad

3 sweet potatoes (about 300 g/10½ oz. each), peeled

1 tablespoon olive oil

1 teaspoon sea salt flakes

70 g/⅓ cup raw macadamia nuts, roughly chopped

200 g/scant 3 cups baby spinach leaves, washed

Dressing

1 tablespoon cider vinegar

1 teaspoon wholegrain mustard

2 tablespoons macadamia or olive oil

sea salt and freshly ground black pepper

Serves 4

Preheat the oven to 190°C (375°F) Gas 5.

Cut the sweet potatoes into 2-cm/¾-inch cubes and toss in a bowl with the olive oil and salt flakes. Tip onto a baking sheet and roast in the preheated oven for 10 minutes.

Put the macadamia nuts in the bowl and toss with any residual oil. Add to the sweet potatoes and roast in the hot oven for 10 minutes, giving the sweet potatoes 20 minutes in total.

To make the dressing, mix together the vinegar, mustard and macadamia oil in a small bowl. Season to taste with salt and pepper. Arrange the spinach leaves on a serving platter and top with the sweet potatoes and macadamia nuts. Spoon the dressing over the top of the salad and serve immediately.

pork and lentil salad

200 g/¾ cup Puy or French green lentils

1 teaspoon Dijon mustard

2 tablespoons balsamic vinegar

½ teaspoon sea salt

½ teaspoon freshly ground black pepper

4 tablespoons extra virgin olive oil

250 g/2 cups button mushrooms

1 tablespoon olive oil

finely grated zest of 1 lemon

2 garlic cloves, crushed

2 tablespoons rosemary needles, chopped

350-g/12-oz. piece of pork eye fillet

100 ml/⅓ cup red wine

100 g/1⅓ cups baby spinach leaves, washed

16 cherry tomatoes, halved

Serves 4

Put the lentils in a saucepan with plenty of cold water. Bring to the boil, then reduce to a simmer and cook for 20 minutes. Drain and set aside.

In a large bowl, whisk together the mustard, vinegar and ¼ teaspoon each of salt and pepper, then whisk in the extra virgin olive oil. Add the mushrooms and lentils and toss to coat. Set aside to marinate.

In a small bowl, mix together the olive oil, lemon zest, garlic, rosemary and remaining ¼ teaspoon each of salt and pepper. Rub this mixture all over the pork fillets.

Heat a frying pan to medium, add the pork and cook for 5 minutes on each side. Remove the pork from the pan to a chopping board and leave to rest for 5 minutes, then slice.

Pour the wine into the hot frying pan and let it bubble, stirring in any marinade left in the pan. Pour this over the lentils and mushrooms. Add the sliced pork to the lentils and mushrooms along with the spinach leaves and cherry tomatoes and toss to combine. Serve immediately.

bacon, egg and bean salad with grilled chorizo on toast

250 g/2 cups fresh broad/fava beans

200 g/7 oz. bacon slices

6 eggs, at room temperature

3 tablespoons freshly squeezed lemon juice

½ teaspoon sugar

¼ teaspoon sea salt

freshly ground black pepper

6 tablespoons extra virgin olive oil

6 chorizo sausages

200 g/scant 3 cups baby spinach leaves, washed

6 slices of crusty bread, such as ciabatta, toasted

Serves 6

Bring a saucepan of water to the boil and add the beans. Return the water to the boil, then cook the beans for 2 minutes until tender. Drain, refresh in iced water to cool and peel if necessary.

Heat a frying pan, add the bacon and cook until crisp. Cut into pieces and set aside.

Fill a saucepan with water, add the eggs and place over a medum/high heat. Bring to the boil and then continue to boil for 2 minutes (6 minutes if you would like hard-boiled eggs). Drain and refresh with cold water. When cool enough to handle, peel and set aside.

In a large bowl, whisk together the lemon juice, sugar, salt, pepper and oil and set aside. Add the spinach and toss to coat. Set aside.

Preheat the grill/broiler to hot. Cut the chorizo into slices and put under the hot grill/broiler for 5 minutes, turning once, until heated through.

To serve, arrange the dressed spinach, broad/fava beans and bacon on plates. Cut the eggs into halves or quarters and place on the plates. Top each piece of toast with the chorizo slices and serve with the salad.

slow-cooked lamb salad with beans, pomegranate and fresh mint

2 tablespoons light olive oil

1 tablespoon sea salt

1 tablespoon ground cumin

2 kg/4 lbs. 8 oz. lamb shoulder

500 g/4 cups fresh broad/fava beans

leaves from a bunch of fresh mint

about 120 g/1 cup pomegranate seeds

2 tablespoons extra virgin olive oil

2 tablespoons freshly squeezed lemon juice

sea salt and freshly ground black pepper

a rack set over a baking sheet or roasting pan

Serves 4

Preheat the oven to 160°C (325°F) Gas 3. Rub the oil then the salt and cumin all over the lamb. Sit the lamb on a rack set over a large baking sheet and cook in the preheated oven for 6 hours. Remove, lightly cover with foil and let rest for up to 3 hours.

Cook the broad/fava beans in a large saucepan of boiling water for 10 minutes, until just tender. Drain well.

Use a fork or your fingers to shred the lamb off of the bone. Transfer to a bowl and add the broad/fava beans, mint, pomegranate seeds, extra virgin olive oil and lemon juice. Toss to combine, season to taste with salt and pepper and serve immediately.

Spanish bread salad with chickpeas, chorizo and baby spinach

Hidden in chorizo are spices that can be enticed out and used to flavour the oil it is cooked in. The warm, spiced pan juices are then tossed with the other ingredients so that the heat gently wilts the spinach. If you can't find chorizo, try substituting it with smoked bacon or pancetta and adding a little extra paprika.

4 thick slices sourdough bread
3 tablespoons olive oil
2 garlic cloves, peeled and left whole
2 chorizo sausages, thinly sliced
1 red onion, thinly sliced
½ teaspoon smoked sweet paprika
½ teaspoon dried thyme
400-g/14-oz. can chickpeas, rinsed and well drained
250 g/1½ cups cherry tomatoes, halved
4 handfuls of baby spinach leaves
2 tablespoons freshly squeezed lemon juice
sea salt and freshly ground black pepper

a ridged stovetop griddle/grill pan or heavy cast iron frying pan

Serves 4

Preheat a stovetop griddle/grill pan over high heat.

Trim the crusts off the bread and discard. Brush both sides of the bread lightly with some of the oil. Add to the preheated pan and cook until golden and slightly charred on both sides. Rub the garlic cloves over the toasted bread and let cool. Tear into large chunks and set aside.

Heat the remaining oil in the pan. Add the chorizo slices and stir-fry for 2–3 minutes, until golden and aromatic. Add the onion, paprika and thyme and cook for 2–3 minutes, until softened. Transfer to a large serving bowl and pour in the seasoned oil from the pan. Add the toasted bread, chickpeas, tomatoes, spinach and lemon juice. Season to taste with salt and pepper and toss well to combine. Serve immediately.

Variation: Smoked tofu makes a good substitute for the chorizo here and tofu or organic vegetarian sausages also work well, if you can find a brand that you like. Simply cook separately, slice and add to the finished dish.

poached chicken and brown rice salad with ginger and lime

Brown rice has a deliciously nutty and wholesome texture and combined in this satisfying salad with Asian flavourings, such as tamari, sesame oil, lime and spicy ginger, it gets a new lease of life.

220 g/1 cup short grain brown rice
1 tablespoon sea salt
5-cm/2-inch piece of fresh ginger, peeled
2 spring onions/scallions
a small bunch of fresh coriander/cilantro
2 skinless chicken breast fillets
leaves from a small bunch of fresh mint
1 tablespoon sesame oil
65 ml/⅓ cup tamari or dark soy sauce
2 tablespoons freshly squeezed lime juice
1 teaspoon sugar
lime wedges, to serve

Serves 4

Put the rice in a large saucepan with plenty of water. Set over high heat, bring to the boil then reduce the heat and cook for about 30 minutes, until tender. Rinse under cold water, drain well and put in a bowl.

Put 3 litres/3 quarts cold water in a saucepan and add the salt. Cut the ginger in half. Thinly slice one half and finely grate the other. Put the sliced ginger in the saucepan with the water and put the grated ginger in a bowl. Roughly chop the spring onions/scallions (green parts only) and add to the pan. Finely chop the white parts and add to the reserved grated ginger. Cut the stems off the coriander/cilantro and add to the water. Roughly chop the coriander/cilantro leaves and add these to the rice.

Bring the water to the boil then add the chicken breasts, making sure they are fully submerged. Cover the pan with a tight-fitting lid and remove from the heat. Let the chicken poach undisturbed, for 45 minutes. Remove from the water and let cool to room temperature.

Add the mint leaves to the rice. Add the sesame oil, tamari, lime juice and sugar to the bowl with the grated ginger and spring onion/scallion whites and stir to combine.

Thinly slice the chicken and add to the rice mixture. Add the dressing, stir to combine and serve immediately with lime wedges for squeezing on the side.

blue cheese and steak winter salad

250 g/9 oz. lean steak, trimmed of any fat

extra virgin olive oil

1 onion, thinly sliced

about 1 tablespoon balsamic vinegar

75 g/⅓ cup cherry tomatoes

55 g/⅔ cup rocket/arugula

60 g/2¼ oz. Stichelton or Stilton, rind removed

sea salt and freshly ground black pepper

Serves 2

Lay the steak on a sheet of parchment paper on a chopping board, cover with another sheet of parchment paper and beat with a meat mallet or rolling pin. Rub a little olive oil into both sides of the steak and season lightly with salt and pepper. Heat a ridged stovetop griddle/grill pan until almost smoking, then lay the steak in the pan and cook for 1 minute. Turn and cook for 1 minute on the other side, then transfer from the pan to a plate.

Turn down the heat under the pan slightly, smear a little oil over the onion slices and place them in a single layer in the pan. Cook for a couple of minutes until beginning to turn dark brown, then carefully turn and cook the other side. Set aside on another plate and drizzle over a little of the balsamic vinegar.

Finally, tip the cherry tomatoes into the pan with a little extra oil, if necessary, and roll them around until the skins begin to burst.

Cut the steak into fine slices with a sharp knife. Divide the rocket/arugula between 2 plates, top with the onions and arrange the tomatoes around the plate. Scatter over the steak slices and crumble over the cheese. Trickle over a little extra oil and balsamic vinegar and season with pepper. Serve immediately with crusty bread.

roast duck, sausage, sweet potato and cherry salad

4 duck legs

3 tablespoons olive oil

½ teaspoon ground cinnamon

3 sweet potatoes (about 200 g/7 oz. each), peeled

1 teaspoon sea salt flakes

8 thin sausages, duck or pork

1 tablespoon sherry vinegar or cider vinegar

finely grated zest of 1 orange and 2 tablespoons freshly squeezed juice

1 tablespoon clear honey

1 teaspoon Dijon mustard

4 tablespoons extra virgin olive oil

1 frisée lettuce, leaves separated

24 cherries, halved and pitted

Serves 4

Preheat the oven to 180°C (350°F) Gas 4.

Slash the duck legs a few times through the flesh. Put 2 tablespoons of the olive oil in a small bowl and whisk in the cinnamon. Use your fingers to rub the oil into the duck. Put the duck in a roasting pan and roast in the preheated oven for 1 hour, turning occasionally.

Cut the sweet potatoes into 2-cm/¾-inch cubes and toss in a bowl with the remaining olive oil and ½ teaspoon of the salt flakes.

Remove the duck from the roasting pan and set aside to cool. Pour most of the rendered fat off the roasting pan and discard. Add the sausages and sweet potatoes to the roasting pan and coat with the little fat left from the duck. Roast for 30 minutes, stirring twice. Remove from the oven and let cool. Cut the sausages into quarters. Slice the meat from the duck legs.

In a bowl, whisk together the vinegar, orange zest and juice, honey, mustard and remaining ½ teaspoon salt flakes. Slowly whisk in the extra virgin olive oil until incorporated.

Arrange the frisée lettuce on a serving plate. Top with the duck, sausages, sweet potatoes and cherries. Pour over the dressing and serve immediately.

hot smoked salmon and cannellini bean salad with gremolata

leaves from a bunch each of fresh flat-leaf parsley and fresh mint, roughly chopped

1 clove garlic, crushed

1 teaspoon grated lemon zest

2 tablespoons freshly squeezed lemon juice

65 ml/¼ cup extra virgin olive oil

400 g/14 oz. hot smoked salmon fillet

400-g/14-oz. can cannellini beans, drained and well rinsed

2 small red onions, thinly sliced

1 cucumber, peeled, halved and sliced

50 g/⅔ cup baby spinach leaves

sea salt and freshly ground black pepper

Serves 4

To make the gremolata, combine the parsley, mint, garlic, lemon zest and juice and oil in a small bowl.

Roughly flake the salmon into a large bowl and add the beans, onions, cucumber and spinach leaves. Season to taste with salt and pepper and toss to combine. Serve immediately with the gremolata on the side as a spooning sauce.

Variation: Replace the salmon with 400 g/14 oz. firm tofu or tempeh (an Indonesian speciality that has a nuttier, more savoury flavour than tofu), cut into thin slivers, and add a handful of roughly chopped fresh coriander/cilantro leaves for extra flavour.

indulgent treats

Baking is such a satisfying and comforting pastime. Make a batch of brownies or bars so that the family can help themselves during the week, or keep a jar of delicious home-baked cookies hidden away to offer to visitors who come in from the cold.

cherry marzipan streusel squares

These are also great made with raspberry or plum jam/jelly.

100 g/¾ cup plain/all-purpose flour
50 g/3 tablespoons butter, chilled and diced
1 tablespoon icing/confectioners' sugar
5 tablespoons cherry jam/jelly

Streusel topping

75 g/⅔ cup plain/all-purpose flour
75 g/½ cup granulated sugar
25 g/2 tablespoons butter, softened and cubed
50 g/1¾ oz. marzipan, diced
50 g/⅓ cup undyed glacé/candied cherries, chopped
50 g/½ cup flaked almonds

Almond layer

100 g/6½ tablespoons butter, softened and cubed
75 g/½ cup granulated sugar
2 large eggs, lightly beaten
100 g/⅔ cup ground almonds
25 g/3 tablespoons plain/all-purpose flour

an 18-cm/7-inch square pan, ideally loose-based, greased

Makes 12

For the pastry, put the flour, butter and sugar in an electric mixer and whiz until the mixture resembles breadcrumbs. Add 2 tablespoons cold water and whiz again. Add a few more drops of water, if needed, to bring together into a dough.

Tip the dough out on a lightly floured work surface and roll out until it is about 3–4 mm/⅛ inch thick. Trim the edges with a sharp knife to make a 19-cm/7½-inch square. Line the base of the pan with the dough – it will come slightly up the inside of the pan all the way round. Refrigerate for 30 minutes.

Preheat the oven to 200°C (400°F) Gas 6.

To make the streusel topping, tip the flour and sugar into the electric mixer (or use a mixing bowl and an electric whisk) and whiz together. Add the butter and whiz until the mixture is crumbly. Tip into a bowl, if necessary, and stir in the marzipan, cherries and flaked almonds.

To make the almond layer, mix all the ingredients together in the electric mixer until amalgamated.

Spread the jam/jelly on top of the pastry base. Spoon blobs of the almond mixture on top of the jam/jelly and spread with a spatula. Scatter the streusel topping over the top. Put the pan on a baking sheet and bake in the preheated oven for 40 minutes, or until lightly golden. Cover with foil towards the end of cooking to prevent over-browning. Leave to cool in the pan before cutting into 12 squares.

hazelnut cheesecake bars

These bars will keep in the refrigerator for a day or so. They are ideal for coffee time or they also double up well as a simple dessert served with poached fruit.

200 g/1½ cups shelled, blanched whole hazelnuts
75 g/5 tablespoons butter
200 g/6½ oz. ginger nut biscuits/gingersnaps, broken into pieces
icing/confectioners' sugar, for dusting

Cheesecake topping

400 g/14 oz. cream cheese
175 g/¾ cup granulated sugar
3 large eggs
300 ml/1¼ cups crème fraîche/sour cream

a 20 x 33-cm/9 x 13-inch baking pan, greased

Makes 14

Preheat the oven to 180°C (350°F) Gas 4.

Spread the hazelnuts on a baking sheet and toast in the preheated oven for 10–12 minutes, then leave to cool. Reduce the oven temperature to 160°C (325°F) Gas 3.

Melt the butter in a small pan and leave to cool slightly.

Tip the biscuits/gingersnaps into a food processor. Add half the cooled hazelnuts and whiz together until you have fine crumbs. Add the melted butter and briefly whiz again. Tip the mixture into the prepared baking pan and press down firmly with the back of a spoon to make an even layer. Put the pan on a baking sheet.

To make the cheesecake topping, put all the ingredients in an electric mixer (or use a large mixing bowl and an electric whisk) and whisk to combine. Carefully pour the mixture on top of the biscuit/cookie base in the pan – the mixture will come pretty near the top. Roughly chop the remaining hazelnuts and scatter over the cheesecake. Bake in the preheated oven for 45 minutes. Leave to cool completely.

Refrigerate for 30 minutes before cutting into 14 bars with a sharp knife. The cheesecake will be soft-set. Lightly dust with icing/confectioners' sugar.

We're proud to offer a selection of produce from our Avebury farm & artisan suppliers across the South West, including goat milk, meat, cheese, soaps, gifts and much more!
Our Farm Shop and Kitchen is also home to delicious lunches, hot & cold drinks and sweet treats!

Visit Us

Come and shop our range of all things goat & enjoy a light lunch or coffee

Indoor tables or alfresco seating in our open goat shed

Opening Hours

Monday & Tuesday - Closed

Wednesday to Sunday
& Bank Holidays:
9am til 4pm

opening hours subject to seasonal change

Just 1 mile from Avebury Stone Circle - pop in and see us when you visit!

Find us on the A4361 towards Swindon

shop online at www.thegourmetgoatfarmer.co.uk

no-bake chocolate, macadamia and fig slices

100 g/6½ tablespoons unsalted butter

2 tablespoons clear honey

300 g/10 oz. dark/bittersweet chocolate (50–70% cocoa solids), broken into pieces

100 g/3½ oz. milk chocolate, broken into pieces

6 digestive or other sweetmeal biscuits/graham crackers

100 g/⅔ cup shelled macadamia nuts

100 g/⅔ cup ready-to-eat dried figs

cocoa powder, for dusting

an 18-cm/7-inch square pan, ideally loose-based, greased

Makes 16

Put the butter, honey and both types of chocolate in a medium pan and melt gently, stirring from time to time.

Meanwhile, roughly chop the biscuits/crackers, nuts and figs. Stir into the melted chocolate mixture.

Tip the mixture into the prepared pan. Leave to cool completely before refrigerating for 2–3 hours to set. Cut into 16 slices.

white chocolate and coffee truffle brownies

240 g/8 oz. dark/bittersweet chocolate (at least 70% cocoa solids)

100 g/6½ tablespoons unsalted butter

2 teaspoons instant coffee granules

3 tablespoons boiling water

3 eggs

135 g/⅔ cup golden caster/granulated sugar

55 g/½ cup plain/all-purpose flour

70 g/2½ oz. white chocolate, chopped (or use chips)

cocoa powder, to dust

an 18-cm/7-inch square brownie pan (3 cm/1¼ inch deep), lined with parchment paper

Makes about 9 squares

Preheat the oven to 150°C (300°F) Gas 2.

Put the chocolate and butter in a heatproof bowl over a saucepan of barely simmering water. Do not let the base of the bowl touch the water. Stir until melted. Set aside to cool.

Put the instant coffee and boiling water in a cup and stir until dissolved. Set aside.

Put the eggs and sugar in a mixing bowl and whisk until pale and creamy. Stir in the coffee. Sift in the flour and fold in gently, then fold in the molten chocolate and mix until smooth. Finally, stir in the chopped chocolate.

Pour the batter into the prepared baking pan and bake in the preheated oven for about 15 minutes. The brownies should have risen slightly. Leave to cool completely, then dust with cocoa powder. Cut into 9 squares and serve.

chocolate sea salt cookies

140 g/⅓ cup plain/all-purpose flour

40 g/½ cup cocoa powder

½ teaspoon baking powder

½ teaspoon bicarbonate of soda/baking soda

120 g/12 oz. dark/bittersweet chocolate (70% cocoa solids), roughly chopped

170 g/1½ sticks unsalted butter, at room temperature

85 g/⅓ cup dark brown soft sugar

40 g/¼ cup granulated sugar

1 egg

1 teaspoon vanilla extract

1 teaspoon rum

fleur de sel, to sprinkle

2 baking sheets, lined with greaseproof paper

Makes approximately 24

Preheat the oven to 180°C (350°F) Gas 4.

Sift together the flour, cocoa powder, baking powder and bicarbonate of soda/baking soda. Melt 40 g/4 oz. of the chocolate, either in a bowl set over a pan of simmering water or a microwave. Cream together the butter and sugars in a food processor on high speed until light and fluffy. Add the egg, vanilla extract, rum and melted chocolate. Beat for 2 minutes, then reduce the speed to slow and add the flour mixture. When mixed, stir in the remaining chocolate.

Put the mixture in the refrigerator for 5 minutes to harden slightly. Scoop tablespoons of the mixture onto the lined baking sheets, 5 cm/2 inches apart (a small ice cream scoop is good for this). Flatten slightly with the back of the scoop. Sprinkle a little fleur de sel on top of each cookie and bake in the preheated oven for 10 minutes.

chocolate heaven muffins

75 g/5 tablespoons butter

75 g/2½ oz. dark/bittersweet chocolate (about 50% cocoa solids)

75 g/2½ oz. milk chocolate

50 g/2 oz. white chocolate

100 g/½ cup crème fraîche/sour cream

50 ml/3 tablespoons milk

50 g/¼ cup light brown soft sugar

2 large eggs

175 g/1½ cups plain/all-purpose flour

2 tablespoons cocoa powder

1 tablespoon baking powder

a pinch of salt

1 tablespoon demerara/light brown soft sugar

a 6-hole muffin pan, lined with paper muffin cases

Makes 6

Preheat the oven to 200°C (400°F) Gas 6.

Melt the butter in a small pan and leave to cool slightly.

Chop the three types of chocolate into small chunks.

In a large mixing bowl and using a balloon whisk, whisk together the crème fraîche/sour cream, milk, light brown soft sugar, eggs and melted butter.

Sift in the flour, cocoa and baking powder. Sprinkle in the salt and add all the chopped chocolate. Using a large metal spoon, fold everything together until combined, but don't over-mix.

Divide the mixture between the muffin cases. Sprinkle each muffin with a little demerara/light brown soft sugar. Bake the muffins in the preheated oven for 20 minutes – by which time they will be risen, but still very slightly unset in the middle. They will continue to cook as they cool.

mini chocolate and cherry cakes

Using beetroot/beets in these cakes gives them slightly soft centres and they freeze well, before decorating. If you are making them as a gift, dust the tops with cocoa, then sprinkle with edible mini gold balls – dip the end of your finger in a little cold water before applying so that they stick.

75 g/2½ oz. dark/bittersweet chocolate (about 50% cocoa solids)
50 g/⅓ cup dried sour cherries (or dried cranberries)
175 g/1⅓ cups self-raising/rising flour
40 g/⅓ cup cocoa powder
175 g/¾ cup light brown soft sugar
250 ml/1 cup groundnut or vegetable oil
3 large eggs
a pinch of salt
150 g/5 oz. cooked, peeled beetroot/beets

a 9-hole petite loaf pan (holes measuring 5.5 x 8 cm/ 2½ x 3⅛ inch and 2.5 cm/1 inch deep), lined with paper mini-loaf liners

Makes 9

Preheat the oven to 180°C (350°F) Gas 4.

Break the chocolate into pieces and melt it in a heatproof bowl set over a pan of barely simmering water. Leave to cool slightly.

Roughly chop the sour cherries.

Sift the flour into an electric mixer (or use a large mixing bowl and an electric whisk). Add the cocoa, sugar, oil, eggs, salt and the melted chocolate, and whisk until combined. Using the coarse side of a grater, grate the beetroot/beets into the mixture and sprinkle in the chopped sour cherries. Using a large metal spoon, fold everything together gently.

Divide the mixture between the loaf cases. Bake in the preheated oven for 20–25 minutes, or until well risen. Leave the cakes to cool completely in the pan.

rhubarb custard and crumble tartlets

500 g/1 lb. 2 oz. ready made sweet shortcrust pastry

Crumble
100 g/¾ cup plain/all-purpose flour
50 g/3 tablespoons unsalted butter, chilled and cubed
40 g/3 tablespoons sugar

Rhubarb custard
360 g/12 oz. rhubarb, trimmed and chopped into small pieces
130 g/⅔ cup golden caster/granulated sugar
3 eggs
a few drops of pure vanilla extract
130 ml/½ cup double/heavy cream

a baking sheet, lined with parchment paper and 6 x 9-cm/ 2½ x 3½-inch loose-based fluted tartlet pans, greased

Makes 6

Preheat the oven to 180°C (350°F) Gas 4.

To make the crumble, mix the flour, butter and sugar in a food processor. Bring the dough together with your hands and transfer to a lightly floured surface. Roll with a rolling pin until about 3 mm/⅛ inch thick, then place on the prepared baking sheet. Bake in the preheated oven for 15 minutes, or until pale gold. Remove from the oven (leaving the oven on) and leave to cool completely, then crush into crumbs and set aside.

Line the tartlet pans with the pastry and trim the excess neatly around the edges. Blind bake for 10 minutes, or until pale gold. Leave the oven on.

To make the rhubarb custard, put the rhubarb in a roasting pan, sprinkle over the sugar and give it a stir. Cover with foil and roast in the hot oven for about 20–25 minutes, until soft. Remove from the oven, leave to cool for a few minutes, then blitz roughly in a food processor or mash with a fork.

Reduce the oven temperature to 150°C (300°F) Gas 2.

Whisk the eggs and vanilla together. Pour the cream into a saucepan over low heat and gently bring to the boil, stirring frequently. Remove from the heat and whisk in the eggs and vanilla and then the rhubarb until well combined.

Fill each tartlet shell up to the top with rhubarb custard and bake in the hot oven for 15–20 minutes, until the filling no longer wobbles when you shake the tartlet. Remove from the oven and scatter crumble over the top. Leave to cool slightly before serving or, even better, serve chilled.

Apples and pears are two of the best-loved fruits the autumn has to offer. Grown in seemingly endless varieties, they are as versatile and delicious to cook with as they are beautiful to look at.

pear, mascarpone and orange tarts

Using ready made and ready-rolled puff pastry makes life easy here. Slices of plum or dessert apple would also work well as a topping for these tarts.

300 g/10 oz. chilled ready made, ready-rolled puff pastry
40 g/3 tablespoons butter
125 g/½ cup mascarpone
3 tablespoons granulated sugar, plus extra for sprinkling
finely grated zest of 1 small orange
75 g/¾ cup ground almonds
1 large egg yolk
4 ripe but firm small pears, cored and thinly sliced (no need to peel)
3–4 tablespoons smooth apricot jam/jelly
4 tablespoons toasted flaked almonds

2–3 large baking sheets, lined with parchment paper and oiled

Makes 12

Preheat the oven to 220°C (425°F) Gas 7 and take the pastry out of the refrigerator.

Melt the butter in a small pan and leave to cool slightly.

Put the mascarpone, sugar, orange zest, ground almonds and egg yolk in a bowl and mix. Refrigerate until needed.

Halve the pastry and roll one half out on a lightly floured work surface until it is about 3–4 mm/⅛ inch – any thicker than that and the pastry won't crisp up in the oven. Trim the edges with a sharp knife to make a 21 x 24-cm/8 x 9½ -inch piece, then cut that into six 7 x 12-cm/3 x 4½-inch rectangles. Arrange the rectangles on one of the prepared baking sheets.

Repeat with the other half of the pastry.

Brush the edges of each rectangle with the melted butter and sprinkle a little sugar over them. Put 2 teaspoons of the mascarpone mixture in the centre of each rectangle. Spread the mixture out using a small knife, leaving a border of about 1 cm/½ inch all the way round.

Top each tart with overlapping slices of pear and scatter a little more sugar over the top. Bake the tarts in the preheated oven for 15 minutes, or until the pastry is golden and crisp. Transfer to a wire rack.

Warm the apricot jam/jelly in a small pan, then use to brush over the pear slices. Sprinkle the flaked almonds over the top, then leave to cool.

pecan and bourbon tartlets

Nutty, with the subtle flavor of Bourbon coming through, these smart, irresistible little tarts are perfect for winter entertaining. Bake a batch at Christmastime to round off a festive feast.

500 g/1 lb. 2 oz. ready made sweet shortcrust pastry
18 pecan halves, to decorate

Date sponge
60 g/2 oz. Medjool dates, pitted
30 ml/2 tablespoons double/heavy cream
1 tablespoon water
30 g/2 tablespoons unsalted butter, melted
30 g/2½ tablespoons light brown soft sugar
1 egg
a few drops of vanilla extract
55 g/½ cup plain/all-purpose flour
1 teaspoon baking powder

Pecan Bourbon filling
1 tablespoon Bourbon whiskey
40 g/3 tablespoons light brown soft sugar
55 ml/¼ cup golden/corn syrup
1 egg, beaten
20 g/1½ tablespoons unsalted butter, melted
60 g/½ cup shelled pecan nuts, roughly chopped

6 x 9-cm/2½ x 3½-inch loose-based fluted tartlet pans, greased

Makes 6

Preheat the oven to 180°C (350°F) Gas 4.

Line the tartlet pans with the pastry and trim the excess around the edges. Refrigerate while you make the filling.

To make the date filling, blitz the dates to a paste in a food processor or simply chop them very finely. Mix with the cream and water and set aside. Put the butter and sugar in a mixing bowl and mix well, then add the egg, vanilla, flour and baking powder. Add date mixture and fold in well.

Remove the tartlet shells from the refrigerator and spoon about 1½ tablespoons of the date filling into them. Bake in the preheated oven for 15 minutes, then remove from the oven (leaving the oven on).

In the meantime, make the pecan Bourbon filling. Put the Bourbon, sugar and syrup in a mixing bowl and mix well. Add the egg, mix well, then stir in the melted butter and pecan nuts.

Spoon the pecan Bourbon filling on top of the tartlets and spread evenly. Decorate with 3 pecan halves and return to the oven for another 10 minutes. Remove from the oven and leave to cool before serving.

chocolate and chestnut tart

Chocolate shortcrust pastry
25 g/1¾ cups plain/all-purpose flour
25 g/3 tablespoons cocoa powder
125 g/1 stick unsalted butter, chilled and cubed
85 g/5 tablespoons golden caster/granulated sugar
1 egg

Chestnut filling
35 g/2 tablespoons unsalted butter, at room temperature
35 g/2 tablespoons golden caster/granulated sugar
1 egg
60 g/½ cup plain/all-purpose flour
1 teaspoon baking powder
30 g/1 oz. cooked chestnuts, chopped
35 ml/3 tablespoons double/heavy cream, chilled
2 tablespoons cold water
90 g/3 oz. canned sweetened chestnut purée

Chocolate ganache
50 g/1½ oz. milk chocolate, finely chopped
50 g/1½ oz. dark/bittersweet chocolate, finely chopped
190 ml/¾ cup double/heavy cream

a 23-cm/9-inch loose-based fluted tart pan, greased

Makes about 8 slices

Preheat the oven to 180°C (350°F) Gas 4.

To make the pastry, put the flour, cocoa, butter and sugar in a mixer and blitz until you get crumbs. Add the egg and mix again. Take the dough out of the mixer and bring together into a ball. Put the dough on a lightly floured surface and roll with a rolling pin until 3–4 mm/¼ inch thick. Line the tart pan with the pastry and chill in the refrigerator while you prepare the filling.

To make the chestnut filling, cream the butter and sugar in a mixing bowl until light and fluffy. Add the egg and mix well. Mix the flour, baking powder and chestnuts together in a separate bowl, then mix into the wet ingredients. Finally, slowly add the cream and water and incorporate well.

Remove the tart shell from the refrigerator and spread the chestnut purée over the base. Spoon the chestnut sponge on top and spread evenly. Bake in the preheated oven for 20 minutes, or until the dough has risen and is pale gold. Remove from the oven and leave to cool for a few minutes. Trim the top of the filling if it has risen too much.

To make the chocolate ganache, put the chocolate in a mixing bowl. Put the cream in a saucepan and gently bring to the boil over low heat, stirring frequently. Pour into the mixing bowl and whisk until you get a smooth cream. Leave to cool for 10 minutes, then pour it into the tart. Refrigerate and serve chilled.

pear and almond tart

1 part-baked sweet shortcrust pastry case, 27 cm/10½ inches diameter or 500 g/1 lb. 2 oz. ready made ready-rolled shortcrust pastry, part-baked in a 35 x 12-cm/14 x 4½-inch tart pan (as shown above)

100 g/7 tablespoons unsalted butter, softened

100 g/½ cup granulated sugar

2 large eggs

100 g/⅔ cup ground almonds

2 tablespoons plain/all-purpose flour

1 teaspoon vanilla extract

3–4 ripe pears, sliced

vanilla ice cream or custard sauce, to serve

Serves 6

Preheat the oven to 190°C (375°F) Gas 5.

In a mixing bowl, combine the butter and sugar and beat with a hand-held electric whisk until light and fluffy. Add the eggs one at a time, beating well with each addition. Add the almonds, flour and vanilla seeds and mix just to combine.

Spread the almond mixture in the pastry case in an even layer. Arrange the pear slices on top. Bake in the preheated oven until puffed and golden, about 20–25 minutes. Serve warm with vanilla ice cream or custard sauce.

tarte tatin

500 g/1 lb. 2 oz. ready made puff pastry

150 g/1 stick plus 2 tablespoons unsalted butter

150 g/¾ cup granulated sugar

1.5 kg/3 lbs. (about 9) Golden Delicious or tart apples such as Cox's, peeled, cored and quartered

crème fraîche/sour cream, to serve

a heavy flameproof tart tatin pan (ideally enamelled cast iron or lined copper), 20 cm/7½ inches diameter

Serves 6

Roll out the pastry on a floured work surface to a round the diameter of the pan; turn the pan upside-down on the rolled out dough and trace around it with the tip of a sharp knife. Transfer the pastry round to a baking sheet and chill until needed.

Put the butter and sugar in the tart tatin pan and set over high heat. Melt, stirring continuously to blend. Remove from the heat and arrange the apple quarters in the pan in 2 circles. The inner circle should go in the opposite direction to the outer circle.

Return to the heat and cook for about 30 minutes. From this point, watch the apples carefully and cook for a further 5–15 minutes, until the liquid thickens and turns a golden caramel color.

Preheat the oven to 200°C (400°F) Gas 6.

Remove the pan from the heat and top with the pastry round, gently tucking in the edges. Transfer to the preheated oven and bake until browned, about 45–60 minutes. Remove from the oven and let cool only slightly. Unmold while still warm or the caramel will harden making it too difficult. To do this, carefully invert the tart onto a serving plate so that the pastry is on the bottom. Serve hot, warm or at room temperature with crème fraîche/sour cream.

Dutch apple pie

There are several different ways to top this alternative to a classic American apple pie, including a lattice crust or this streusel topping, which is not strictly speaking Dutch as it comes from the Amish communities of America.

500 g/1 lb. 2 oz. ready made shortcrust pastry
1.3 kg/3 lbs. eating apples, such as Cox's, Braeburn, Jonagold or Golden Delicious
100 g/½ cup granulated sugar
100 g/¾ cup sultanas/golden raisins
1 teaspoon ground cinnamon
1 tablespoon freshly squeezed lemon juice
whipped cream, to serve

For the streusel topping
90 g/½ cup light brown soft sugar
45 g/½ cup plus 2 tablespoons plain/all-purpose flour
120 g/1 stick unsalted butter, chilled
1 teaspoon each cinnamon, nutmeg and allspice
a pinch of fine sea salt
80 g/½ cup walnuts, chopped

a springform cake pan, 24 cm/9½ inches diameter, buttered and floured

Serves 6–8

Preheat the oven to 180°C (350°F) Gas 4.

Roll out the pastry on a floured work surface and line the pan with the pastry, all the way up the sides to the top edge. Let chill. Refrigerate while you prepare the apples.

Peel, core and dice the apples and put them in a bowl. Add the sugar, sultanas/golden raisins, cinnamon and lemon juice and mix well using your hands.

In a food processor, combine all the topping ingredients, except the walnuts, and process to form coarse crumbs. Add the walnuts and pulse just a few times to combine.

Put the apple mixture in the pastry-lined pan. Sprinkle the streusel topping over the top in an even layer, going all the way to the edges and tidy up the edges of the pastry.

Cover with foil and bake in the preheated oven for about 30 minutes. Remove the foil and continue baking for about 25–30 minutes, until the top of the pie is golden.

Remove from the oven and let cool. Serve warm with whipped cream.

classic apple pie

Apple pie afficionados believe that the best pies are made with a variety of apples to combine sweet and tart flavours with firm and melting textures.

1.3 kg/3 lbs. mixed apples, such as Cox's, Braeburn Golden Delicious, Jonagold, Honeycrisp and Granny Smith, peeled and cored
50 g/¼ cup granulated sugar, or more to taste
1 teaspoon ground cinnamon
1 tablespoon freshly squeezed lemon juice
single/light cream, to serve

For the pastry
300 g/2 cups plus 2 tablespoons plain/all-purpose flour
1 teaspoon granulated sugar
¼ teaspoon fine sea salt
75 g/5 tablespoons unsalted butter
75 g/5 tablespoons lard or vegetable shortening
1 egg yolk
4 tablespoons cold water
1 egg, beaten
sugar, for sprinkling

a pie dish or plate (with sloping sides), 23–25 cm/ 9–10 inches diameter, greased

Serves 6–8

To make the pastry, put the flour, sugar and salt in a food processor and process just to combine. Add the butter and lard and pulse until the mixture just forms coarse crumbs. Add the egg yolk and water and pulse again; the mixture should be crumbly but not holding together.

Transfer to a floured work surface and form into a ball. Cut in half, wrap well in clingfilm/plastic wrap and chill for at least 1 hour (if leaving longer, double wrap as dough dries out easily). Roll out half of the dough and line the base of the dish. Trim the edges leaving a 1 cm/½ inch overhang. Save the trimmings for decoration. Chill while you prepare the apples.

Slice the apples – not too thick and not too thin. Put them in a bowl with the sugar, cinnamon and lemon juice and use your hands to mix well. Transfer to the dough-lined pie dish.

Preheat the oven to 190°C (375°F) Gas 5.

Roll out the remaining dough on a floured work surface to a circle large enough to cover the apples. Brush the edges of the dough in the dish with beaten egg, then lay the other pastry circle on top. Fold over the overhang from the bottom layer and crimp using fingertips, or use the tines of a fork to seal. Decorate as desired and brush lightly with egg, then sprinkle with sugar. Cut 6–8 small slits in the top of the pie.

Put on a baking sheet and bake in the preheated oven until golden, 50–60 minutes. Serve warm with chilled cream.

pear cobbler

A cobbler is a dessert consisting of a sweetened thick batter poured over fruit and baked. Other names for similar recipes are grunt, slump and buckle, but they are all pretty much the same thing. It is a comforting dish, easy to make and even easier to eat!

900 g/1½ lbs. pears, peeled, cored and sliced
75 g/½ cup light brown soft sugar
2 tablespoons plain/all-purpose flour
1 teaspoon vanilla extract
finely grated zest of 1 orange
vanilla ice cream or whipped cream, to serve

For the cobbler batter
300 g/2 cups plain/all-purpose flour
200 g/1 cup sugar
1 tablespoon baking powder
a pinch of fine sea salt
250 ml/1 cup milk
125 g/1 stick plus 1 tablespoon unsalted butter, melted
extra sugar or cinnamon sugar, to sprinkle

an ovenproof baking dish, about 23–25 cm/ 9–10 inches diameter, well-greased

Serves 4–6

Preheat the oven to 190°C (375°F) Gas 5.

In a bowl, combine the pears, sugar, flour, vanilla extract and orange zest. Toss gently with your hands to combine and arrange in an even layer in the bottom of the prepared baking dish. Set aside.

To prepare the cobbler batter, combine the flour, sugar, baking powder and salt in a separate bowl. In a third bowl, stir together the milk and melted butter. Gradually pour the milk mixture into the dry ingredients, beating with a wooden spoon until just smooth.

Drop spoonfuls of the batter on top of the pears, leaving gaps but spreading to the edges. Sprinkle the top with sugar and bake in the preheated oven until golden brown, about 40–50 minutes. Serve warm with vanilla ice cream or whipped cream.

When it's cold outside, there is something so comforting about coming home to a slice of warm apple pie with its crumbly pastry and deliciously sweet filling.

pear clafoutis with figs and almonds

3 ripe pears

3 ripe figs

200 ml/¾ cup crème fraîche/sour cream

200 ml/¾ cup whole milk

3 eggs

125 g/¾ cup granulated sugar

2 tablespoons ground almonds

½ teaspoon ground cinnamon

icing/confectioners' sugar, to dust

single/light cream, to serve

a non-stick baking dish, about 22–25 cm/9–10 inches diameter, well-buttered

Serves 4–6

Preheat the oven to 200°C (400°F) Gas 6.

Peel and core the pears and cut into largeish pieces. Trim the stem ends from the figs and cut into slightly smaller pieces. If there is too much white on the skins, trim this off. Put the fruit in the prepared baking dish and distribute evenly. Set aside.

In a mixing bowl, combine the crème fraîche/sour cream, milk, eggs, sugar, almonds and cinnamon. Mix well with a hand-held electric whisk.

Pour the batter evenly over the fruit and bake in the preheated oven for about 35–45 minutes, until puffed and golden. Let cool slightly and dust with icing/confectioners' sugar just before serving. Serve warm with chilled cream.

apple and blackberry crumble

900 g/2 lbs. mixed apple varieties, peeled, cored and chopped

450 g/1 lb. blackberries

50 g/¼ cup granulated sugar

vanilla ice cream, to serve

For the crumble topping

80 g/1 cup porridge oats

140 g/1 cup plain/all-purpose flour

80 g/½ cup light brown soft sugar

80 g/½ cup ground almonds

½ teaspoon ground cinnamon

150 g/1 stick plus 2 tablespoons unsalted butter, cut into cubes

an ovenproof dish, 23–25 cm/ 9–10 inches diameter, or 4–6 dishes, 9–12 cm/ 3½–4½ inches diameter, well-greased

Serves 4–6

Preheat the oven to 200°C (400°F) Gas 6.

Put the apples, berries and sugar in a mixing bowl and use your hands to mix well. Transfer to the prepared baking dish.

To prepare the topping, combine the oats, flour, sugar, almonds and cinnamon in a bowl and mix well. Add the butter. Using a pastry blender, or fingertips, rub in the butter until the mixture resembles coarse breadcrumbs. Alternatively, use a food processor and blend carefully with the pulse button; do not over-process or you will grind the oats too finely.

Sprinkle the topping evenly over the apple mixture. Bake in the preheated oven until the crumble is golden and the fruit is bubbling, 35–45 minutes. Serve warm with vanilla ice cream.

oaty apple and raisin crumble

A baked fruit crumble, served warm from the oven, has to be one of the most popular winter desserts. Adding oats to a crumble topping makes for a deliciously crunchy texture.

2 tablespoons brandy
1 tablespoon clear honey
50 g/⅓ cup raisins
5 Granny Smith apples, peeled cored and sliced
75 g/½ cup golden caster/granulated sugar
vanilla ice cream or chilled single/light cream, to serve

Crumble topping:
75 g/⅔ cup plain wholemeal/wholewheat flour
30 g/¼ cup rolled oats
½ teaspoon baking powder
½ teaspoon ground cinnamon
75 g/5 tablespoons unsalted butter, chilled and cut into cubes
60 g/5 tablespoons light brown soft sugar

a medium baking dish, greased

Serves 4

Preheat the oven to 200°C (400°F) Gas 6.

Put the brandy, honey and raisins in a small saucepan and set over medium heat. Cook for 5 minutes, stirring constantly, until almost all the liquid has evaporated. Set aside.

Put the apples, sugar and 2 tablespoons cold water in a separate saucepan and set over medium heat. Cover and cook for 10–15 minutes, stirring often, until the apples have softened. Stir in the raisin mixture and let cool. Transfer to the prepared baking dish.

To make the crumble topping, put the flour, oats, baking powder, cinnamon and butter in a bowl. Use your hands to combine all of the ingredients, rubbing the butter between your fingertips, until the mixture resembles coarse sand. Stir in the sugar and sprinkle the mixture evenly over the apple mixture in the baking dish.

Bake in the preheated oven for 25–30 minutes, until the topping is crisp and golden. Serve warm with vanilla ice cream or chilled cream, as preferred.

vanilla rice pudding

1 vanilla bean

1 litre/4 cups whole milk

125 ml/½ cup single/light cream

50 g/½ stick unsalted butter

75 g/⅓ cup golden caster/
granulated sugar

100 g/½ cup short grain
white rice

*a medium heatproof
baking dish*

Serves 4

Preheat the oven to 150°C (300°F) Gas 2.

Roll the vanilla bean between the palms of your hand to
soften. Split it lengthwise with a small sharp knife and use the
tip of the knife to scrape the seeds directly into a bowl. Add
the milk, sugar and cream and whisk well to combine.

Put the butter in the heatproof baking dish and set over
high heat. When the butter is sizzling, add the rice and stir for
1–2 minutes, until it is shiny. Carefully pour the milk mixture
into the dish and use a large spoon to gently stir, breaking up
any large lumps of rice and freeing any grains that are stuck
to the bottom of the dish. Transfer to the preheated oven and
bake, uncovered, for 3 hours, until the top has a golden
brown crust. Let cool slightly before serving.

arctic roll with vanilla and chocolate

This recipe is a classic from the 1970s which really deserves a comeback. It is a great dessert for winter entertaining. Serve it on its own or with cream or hot chocolate sauce on the side.

3 eggs
100 g/½ cup granulated sugar
2 teaspoons baking powder
30 g/⅓ cup cornflour/cornstarch
2 tablespoons cocoa powder
50 g/⅓ cup icing/confectioners' sugar

Filling
1 litre/4 cups vanilla ice cream
50 g/2 oz. dark/bittersweet chocolate, grated

a large baking sheet, lined with non-stick parchment paper

Serves 6–8

Preheat the oven to 200°C (400°F) Gas 6.

Put the eggs and sugar in a large mixing bowl and whisk with a handheld electric whisk until the mixture is foam-like – this will take up to 10 minutes. When it is ready, it will be almost white, have doubled in size and the batter will drop off the beaters in a figure-of-eight when you lift them out of the bowl.

In a separate bowl, sift the baking powder, cornflour/cornstarch and cocoa powder together, then fold into the egg mixture.

Spread the mixture evenly on the prepared baking sheet with a spatula to make a rough square about 30 x 30 cm/ 12 x 12 inches. (The mixture will not spread when it bakes.) Bake in the preheated oven for 10 minutes.

In the meantime, take the ice cream for the filling out of the freezer to soften for about 10 minutes.

Cut a sheet of parchment paper slightly bigger than the baked cake, lay it on the work surface and dust generously with some of the icing/confectioners' sugar. Carefully lift the hot, baked cake from the baking sheet, using the lining parchment paper, and place it face down on the dusted parchment paper. Peel the lining parchment paper away from the cake gently and leave to cool for a few minutes.

Spread the softened ice cream over the cake, scatter the grated chocolate evenly over it, then roll it carefully into a log shape. Freeze for at least 1 hour.

Before serving, neatly trim the ends of the roll, leave to stand for 15 minutes to soften, then dust with icing/ confectioners' sugar.

spiced pear trifle

Trifle is a traditional English dessert but this recipe departs from the classic recipe as it uses spiced poached pears instead of canned peaches. It is easy to make and looks spectacular when assembled in a large glass bowl.

300 g/10 oz. genoese sponge (about one 23–25 cm/ 9–10 inch cake)
4 tablespoons cognac (optional)
4–6 poached pears (see page 150) poaching liquid reserved
250 ml/1 cup whipping cream, whipped
toasted flaked almonds, to top

For the custard
250 ml/1 cup milk
50 ml/¼ cup double/ heavy cream
8 egg yolks
75 g/½ cup sugar
1 teaspoon vanilla extract

a glass serving dish or 4–6 individual serving dishes

Serves 4–6

To make the custard, combine the milk and cream in a saucepan and warm over low heat. Meanwhile, whisk together the egg yolks and sugar in a heatproof bowl. Whisk the warm milk mixture into the egg yolk mixture, then return the mixture to the saucepan, stirring constantly with a wooden spoon, until it thickens. As soon as it thickens, remove from the heat, transfer to a bowl and add the vanilla extract. Stir it into the custard. Cover the surface of the custard closely with parchment paper to prevent a skin from forming and set aside to cool.

When you're ready to serve, cut the sponge cake into pieces and arrange these in the bottom of the serving dish. Drizzle with the cognac (if using) and some reserved pear poaching liquid. Top with the quartered pears, then spoon over some of the custard. Spoon the whipped cream on top, sprinkle with the almonds and serve.

chocolate chestnut brownie torte

This torte has the texture of a brownie, but it is as light as a feather. It doesn't contain any flour, which is an added bonus for anyone with an intolerance to wheat. In addition to being dusted with cocoa, it also looks pretty scattered with chopped marrons glacés – candied chestnuts.

200 g/6½ oz. dark/bittersweet chocolate (70% cocoa solids), broken into pieces
175 g/1½ sticks unsalted butter, cubed
5 large eggs, separated
175 g/¾ cup granulated sugar
a pinch of salt
100 g/3½ oz. canned unsweetened chestnut purée
cocoa powder, for dusting
a few chopped, toasted hazelnuts, to decorate

a 23-cm/9-inch springform pan, 6 cm/2½ inches deep, oiled and base-lined with parchment paper

Serves 8

Preheat the oven to 180°C (350°F) Gas 4.

Put the chocolate and butter in a heatproof bowl set over a pan of barely simmering water. Stir until the chocolate has melted and the mixture is smooth and glossy. Take the bowl off the heat and leave to cool slightly.

Put the egg yolks, 100 g/½ cup of the sugar and the salt in the bowl of an electric mixer (or use a large mixing bowl and an electric whisk) and beat for about 5 minutes, until pale and mousse-like. Mash and stir the chestnut purée with the back of a spoon in a small bowl, to break it up a bit, then whisk it into the egg-yolk mixture.

In a large, clean bowl and using clean beaters, whisk the egg whites until they form stiff peaks. Add the remaining sugar to the egg whites, a quarter at a time, whisking after each addition.

Using a large metal spoon, carefully fold the melted chocolate mixture into the egg-yolk mixture. Finally, fold in the beaten egg whites. Be as gentle as you can so that you keep as much air in the mixture as possible.

Pour the mixture into the prepared pan and bake in the preheated oven for 40–45 minutes, or until well risen. Leave to cool in the pan. It will sink in the middle as it does so, but this is normal.

Transfer the pan to a large serving plate or board and release the side clip. Lift the ring from the torte and carefully slide the cake off the pan base, using a spatula or fish slice. Peel off the base paper. Dust the torte lightly with cocoa powder and scatter the chopped hazelnuts over the top.

pumpkin and cinnamon strudel

Here's the perfect recipe for winter – a crumbly, heavenly strudel made with creamy, sweet pumpkin and a hint of cinnamon. Make this with large sheets of filo/phyllo pastry, available in Middle Eastern shops or the freezer aisle of supermarkets. Just let it defrost for 1 hour before you start. If you can't find such large sheets, simply overlap your sheets to make the correct size and remember that you'll need more to begin with.

a small pie pumpkin, about 220 g/8 oz.
½ teaspoon ground cinnamon
50 g/¼ cup golden granulated sugar
20 ml/1½ tablespoons vegetable oil
3 large sheets of thick filo/phyllo pastry (47 x 32 cm/18 x 13 inches)
icing/confectioners' sugar, to dust

a baking sheet, greased

Makes 6 slices

Preheat the oven to 170°C (325°F) Gas 3.

Peel and deseed the pumpkin, then grate the flesh and squeeze out any excess water. Put in a bowl and mix with the cinnamon and sugar.

Take one sheet of pastry, lay it on the prepared baking sheet and lightly brush with oil. Place a second sheet on top and lightly brush with oil. Repeat with the third sheet.

Spoon the pumpkin filling along one longer side of the sheets, leaving a 2.5-cm/1-inch gap on either side and spreading the filling about 5 cm/2 inches wide. Fold the longer side of the pastry, nearest the filling, about 2.5 cm/1 inch in, then roll the pastry up, tucking in the sides as you go. When the strudel is baking, the filling will soften and some juice might seep out, so tucking in the sides ensures that not too much juice is lost.

Brush the top of the strudel with a little more oil and bake in the preheated oven for 25 minutes, until golden. Remove from the oven and leave to cool for 5 minutes. Dust with icing/confectioners' sugar and serve warm.

A festive strudel topped with a thick dusting of snowy icing/confectioners' sugar makes a beautiful finishing touch to any special holiday meal.

baked apples and pears with dried fruit, honey and hazelnuts

2 apples, preferably Cox's Orange Pippin or Braeburn

1 just-ripe pear, preferably Conference

20 g/2 tablespoons hazelnuts, coarsely chopped

1 tablespoon sultanas/golden raisins

4–5 dried apricots, chopped

ground cinnamon, to dust

about 2 tablespoons unsalted butter

clear honey, to drizzle

plain yogurt, to serve

a non-stick baking dish, large enough to easily hold the fruit

Serves 2

Preheat the oven to 200°C (400°F) Gas 6.

Peel the apples. If necessary, trim the bottoms slightly so that they sit flat. Using a small knife or a corer, remove the cores. With a small spoon, scrape out some apple around the core cavity to allow for more stuffing. Peel the pear, halve and scoop out the core, as for the apple.

In a small bowl, mix the hazelnuts, sultanas/golden raisins and apricots.

Arrange the apples and pears in the baking dish. Stuff the nut mixture into the apple and pear cavities, mounding it at the top. Top each with a light sprinkling of cinnamon and a tablespoon of butter, then drizzle each with 1–2 teaspoons of honey, to taste. Cover with foil.

Bake in the preheated oven for 20 minutes, then remove the foil and continue baking for about 10–15 minutes, until just golden. Divide the apples and pears carefully between serving plates and pour over any pan juices. Serve warm with plain yogurt.

poached pears

a 750 ml/ 25 oz. bottle good red wine

150 g/¾ cup sugar

3 tablespoons clear honey

freshly squeezed juice of 1 lemon

1 cinnamon stick

1 vanilla pod/bean, split lengthwise

1 large piece of orange peel

1 whole clove

1 black peppercorn

4–6 firm pears

sweetened crème fraîche, sour cream, whipped cream or vanilla ice cream, to serve

Serves 4–6

In a saucepan large enough to hold the pears standing upright, combine the wine, sugar, honey, lemon juice, cinnamon stick, vanilla pod, orange peel, clove and peppercorn. Warm over low heat, stirring occasionally until the sugar has dissolved. Remove from the heat.

Peel the pears but leave them whole.

Place the pears in the wine mixture and simmer, uncovered, until tender (test with the tip of a sharp knife). Timing depends on the quantity, size and ripeness of the pears, about 20–35 minutes.

Transfer the pears to a shallow, non-reactive bowl using a large slotted spoon. Continue cooking the poaching liquid over medium heat until it has reduced by half. Let cool, then strain it through a sieve/strainer and pour over the pears. Leave the pears in the liquid, turning them occasionally, for at least 3 hours before serving.

Note: This dessert can be made up to several days in advance and kept refrigerated. Return the pears to room temperature before serving.

brown sugar pavlova with cinnamon cream and pomegranate

4 large egg whites

50 g/¼ cup light brown soft sugar

175 g/generous ¾ cup golden caster/granulated sugar

1 teaspoon cornflour/cornstarch

1 teaspoon white wine vinegar

300 ml/1¼ cups double/heavy or whipping cream

1 tablespoon icing/confectioners' sugar

1½ teaspoons ground cinnamon

125–150 g/¾–1 cup pomegranate seeds

a baking sheet, lined with parchment paper (don't grease it, or your egg whites will collapse!)

Serves 8

Preheat the oven to 140°C (275°F) Gas 1.

Put the egg whites in a large, clean bowl and whisk with an electric whisk (or use an electric mixer) until they form stiff peaks. Add the sugars, a tablespoon at a time, whisking constantly. Add the cornflour/cornstarch and vinegar with the final addition of sugar.

Pile the meringue mixture onto the prepared baking sheet and form into a circle about 22 cm/9 inches in diameter. Make swirls in the meringue with a skewer or the end of a teaspoon. Bake in the preheated oven for 1 hour, then turn the oven off and leave the pavlova in until cold – overnight is ideal.

To finish, whip the cream with the icing/confectioners' sugar and cinnamon to soft peaks. Pile it onto the pavlova and scatter the pomegranate seeds over the top.

orange and poppy seed cake

300 g/2 sticks plus
5 tablespoons butter, softened

250 g/1¼ cups granulated
sugar

3 teaspoons vanilla extract

5 eggs

3 teaspoons baking powder

300 g/2⅓ cups plain/
all-purpose flour

grated zest of 1½ unwaxed
oranges

freshly squeezed juice of
½ orange

1 tablespoon poppy seeds

*an 18-cm/7-inch loose
bottomed/springform cake pan,
greased*

Serves 12–16

Preheat the oven to 180°C (350°F) Gas 4.

Put the butter and sugar in a large mixing bowl and cream
with a wooden spoon or handheld electric whisk until pale
and fluffy. Stir in the vanilla extract. Add the eggs one by
one, whisking well after each addition.

In a separate bowl, sift the baking powder and flour
together, then fold into the egg mixture.

Fold in the orange zest, juice and poppy seeds and mix
until combined.

Spoon the mixture into the prepared cake pan and level
with the back of the spoon.

Bake in the preheated oven for 50–60 minutes, until the
cake is firm to the touch and a skewer inserted into the
middle comes out clean. The cake tastes best the day
after baking and is also suitable for freezing.

ginger cake

300 g/2 sticks plus
5 tablespoons unsalted butter,
softened at room temperature

250 g/1½ cups light brown
soft sugar

3 teaspoons vanilla extract

5 eggs

3 teaspoons baking powder

1½ teaspoons ground
cinnamon

1½ teaspoons ground cloves

3 teaspoons cardamom
seeds, crushed with a pestle
and mortar

1½ teaspoons ground ginger

300 g/2⅓ cups plain/
all-purpose flour

*an 18-cm/7-inch loose-
bottomed/springform
cake pan, greased*

Makes 12–16 slices

Preheat the oven to 180°C (350°F) Gas 4.

Put the butter and sugar in a large mixing bowl and cream
with a wooden spoon or handheld electric whisk until pale
and fluffy. Stir in the vanilla extract. Add the eggs one by
one, whisking well after each addition.

In a separate bowl, sift the baking powder, spices and flour
together, then fold into the egg mixture.

Spoon the mixture into the prepared cake pan and level
the top with the back of the spoon.

Bake in the preheated oven for 50–60 minutes, until the
cake is firm to the touch and a skewer inserted into the
middle comes out clean. The cake tastes best the day
after baking and is also suitable for freezing.

tropical chai pineapple cake

250 g/8 oz. mixed soft dried
tropical fruit, e.g. pineapple,
papaya, mango, melon,
chopped into small chunks

100 g/3½ oz. pitted, soft
dates, chopped into small
chunks

150 g/1 cup raisins

125 g/½ cup dark brown soft
sugar

1 teaspoon bicarbonate of
soda/baking soda

1 tablespoon ground allspice

1 teaspoon freshly grated
nutmeg

1 small cinnamon stick

3 star anise

4 tablespoons dark rum

150 g/10 tablespoons butter,
chopped

3 chai tea bags soaked in
200 ml/¾ cup boiling water

350 g/12 oz. prepared fresh
pineapple, chopped into
small pieces

grated zest of 2 limes

125 g/1 cup plain/all-purpose
flour

125 g/1 cup self-raising/
rising flour

100 g/⅔ cup shelled brazil
nuts, chopped

2 large eggs, lightly beaten

3 tablespoons clear honey

dried pineapple slices,
to decorate

*a 20-cm/8-inch round pan,
9 cm/3½ inches deep, lightly
buttered and base-lined with
parchment paper*

Serves 16

Put the dried fruit and dates into a medium pan with the
raisins, sugar, bicarbonate of soda/baking soda, all the
spices, the rum and butter. Discard the tea bags from the
chai tea and pour that into the pan too. Stir together and
bring the mixture to simmering point over gentle heat.

When the butter has melted, increase the heat and boil the
mixture for 2 minutes exactly, then transfer the contents to
a large mixing bowl. Stir in the pineapple and lime zest and
leave to cool completely, giving it a stir from time to time.

Preheat the oven to 160°C (325°F) Gas 3.

Remove the cinnamon stick and star anise from the mixture.
Sift both flours into the bowl and add the chopped nuts and
beaten eggs. Stir well. Tip the mixture into the prepared pan
and spread it evenly with a spatula. Bake in the preheated
oven for 1¾ hours, or until risen and deep golden brown.
Leave to cool in the pan.

Tip the cold cake out of the pan and peel off the base paper.
Warm the honey in a small saucepan, then use to brush all
over the cake. Decorate with dried pineapple slices.

blackcurrant, berry and hazelnut crumble cake

This recipe also works well using damson jam. Either way, serve with some chilled plain yogurt on the side.

150 g/10 tablespoons butter, softened
175 g/¾ cup granulated sugar
2 large eggs
125 g/1 cup self-raising/rising flour
50 g/⅓ cup polenta/cornmeal
1 teaspoon baking powder
finely grated zest of 1 small unwaxed lemon
50 g/¼ cup plain yogurt
175 g/¾ cup blackcurrant jam/jelly
175 g/1¼ cups raspberries

Crumble topping
100 g/⅔ cup shelled, blanched whole hazelnuts
75 g/⅓ cup light brown soft sugar
75 g butter/5 tablespoons, chilled and cubed
100 g/¾ cup self-raising/rising flour

a 23-cm/9-inch springform pan, 6 cm/2½ inches deep, lightly buttered and base-lined with parchment paper

Serves 12

Preheat the oven to 180°C (350°F) Gas 4.

To make the crumble topping, chop the nuts by hand or pulse them in a food processor – you want them to be roughly chopped. Mix the sugar, butter and flour in an electric mixer until combined, then add 2 dessertspoons cold water and briefly whiz again until the mixture resembles breadcrumbs. Mix in the nuts. Alternatively, you can rub the butter into the flour by hand in a mixing bowl, then stir in the sugar, water and nuts. Set aside.

Put the butter, sugar, eggs, flour, polenta, baking powder, lemon zest and plain yogurt in an electric mixer and mix until combined.

Spoon the mixture into the prepared pan and spread it evenly. Tip the jam into a bowl and mix it with a spoon to loosen it, then put spoonfuls over the top of the cake mixture. Using the tip of a round-bladed knife, gently spread the jam/jelly by lightly swirling it into the top of the cake mixture. Sprinkle a third of the crumble mixture on top, scatter the raspberries over this, then finish with the remaining crumble topping.

Put the pan on a baking sheet and bake in the preheated oven for 1 hour 5 minutes–1 hour 10 minutes, until just set in the middle. Leave to cool in the pan before releasing it, removing the base paper and transferring to a plate or board to slice.

mulled wine and cranberry tea bread

a wine-mulling spice bag
200 ml/¾ cup light, fruity red wine
1 tablespoon clear honey
75 g/½ cup ready-to-eat dried figs
50 g/½ cup crystallized stem ginger
75 g/½ cup whole blanched almonds
50 g/⅓ cup each dried cranberries and dried sour cherries (or use 100 g/⅔ cup sultanas/golden raisins)
100 g/½ cup light brown soft sugar
2 large eggs, lightly beaten
grated zest of 2 oranges
100 g/1 cup fresh cranberries
225 g/1¾ cups self-raising/rising flour
1 teaspoon ground cinnamon
½ teaspoon ground allspice

Topping
75 g/½ cup dried cranberries (or dried sour cherries, or sultanas/ golden raisins)
2 tablespoons freshly squeezed orange juice
4 tablespoons redcurrant jelly

a 19 x 9-cm/8½ x 4½-inch loaf pan, 7 cm/3 inches deep, lightly buttered and base-lined with parchment paper

Serves 12

First make the mulled wine. Put the wine-mulling spice bag in a medium pan with the red wine and honey. Slowly bring to a simmer, stirring occasionally. Leave over very low heat for 5 minutes, then take the pan off the heat and set aside.

Roughly chop the figs, ginger and almonds and mix with the dried cranberries and cherries and the sugar in a mixing bowl. Remove the spice bag from the mulled wine, then pour the warm wine over the dried fruit and leave to soak for 30 minutes.

Preheat the oven to 160°C (325°F) Gas 3.

Stir the beaten eggs, orange zest and the fresh cranberries into the soaked dried fruit. Next, sift in the flour, cinnamon and allspice. Mix together until thoroughly combined.

Spoon the mixture into the prepared loaf pan. Bake in the preheated oven for 55 minutes, by which time the loaf will have risen and slightly shrunk from the sides of the pan. Leave to cool in the pan, then run a table knife around the edge of the pan, tip the loaf out and peel off the base paper.

To make the topping, gently heat the cranberries, orange juice and redcurrant jelly in a small pan over low heat, stirring until the jelly has dissolved.

Brush the top of the loaf with some of the sticky juices from the topping, then spoon the cranberries along the middle of the loaf. Leave to cool before serving.

cranberry, sherry and vine fruit cake

You can serve this cake as an alternative to traditional Christmas cake. It is loaded with sherry-soaked fruits, walnuts and cranberries.

60 g/4 tablespoons unsalted butter, at room temperature
50 g/¼ cup light brown soft sugar
1 tablespoon molasses (or black treacle)
2 small eggs, beaten
60 g/½ cup plain/all-purpose flour
1½ teaspoons baking powder
½ teaspoon ground cinnamon
freshly grated zest of 1 unwaxed orange
50 g/⅓ cup fresh or frozen cranberries
20 g/2 tablespoons shelled walnuts, chopped

Sherry-soaked fruits
100 g/⅔ cup raisins
130 g/¾ cup sultanas/golden raisins
60 g/½ cup mixed peel
3 tablespoons sherry (dry, if possible)
3 tablespoons apple juice

Topping
100 g/½ cup apricot jam/jelly
100 g/⅔ cup fresh or frozen cranberries
80 g/½ cup walnut halves

a 20-cm/8-inch non-stick springform pan

Makes 10–12 slices

Prepare the sherry-soaked fruits at least 24 hours in advance. Put the raisins, sultanas/golden raisins, mixed peel, sherry and apple juice in a bowl. Mix, cover and leave to rest for at least 24 hours.

When you are ready to make the cake, preheat the oven to 180°C (350°F) Gas 4.

Put the butter, sugar and molasses in a mixing bowl and mix well. Fold in the eggs, then add the flour, baking powder, cinnamon, orange zest, cranberries and walnuts. Finally, fold in about 190 g/7 oz. of the soaked fruit, setting the rest aside for the topping. Pour the mixture into the prepared baking pan and bake in the preheated oven for 30 minutes, or until deep golden and springy to the touch. Remove from the oven and leave to cool in the pan.

To make the topping, put the apricot jam/jelly in a saucepan and gently bring to the boil over low heat, stirring frequently. Add the cranberries and cook for a few minutes, until their skins just begin to crack. Remove from the heat and stir in the walnuts and the remaining sherry-soaked fruit. Mix well and spoon on top of the cake. Cover the cake evenly and press very slightly to fix it in place. Leave to rest for a few hours before serving.

apple and carrot bread with walnuts

This is super simple to make. One large loaf goes a long way and keeps well, so it is ideal if you just want something freshly baked around the house for a few days. It is very nice plain, or spread with butter or cream cheese if you are feeling indulgent.

250 g/1¾ cups plain/all-purpose flour
150 g/¾ cup light brown soft sugar
1 tablespoon baking powder
a pinch of fine sea salt
1 teaspoon ground cinnamon
½ teaspoon ground nutmeg
¼ teaspoon each ground ginger and allspice
100 ml/⅓ cup apple juice
75 g/5 tablespoons unsalted butter, melted
2 large eggs, beaten
1 large tart cooking apple, such as Granny Smith's or Bramley's, peeled, cored and grated
100 g/1 cup grated carrot
65 g/½ cup walnuts, coarsely chopped

a 900-g/2-lb. capacity loaf pan, buttered

Serves 6–8

Preheat the oven to 180°C (350°F) Gas 4.

In a mixing bowl, combine the flour, sugar, baking powder, salt, cinnamon, nutmeg, ginger and allspice. Set aside.

In a separate bowl, mix together the apple juice, melted butter and eggs. Gently fold this mixture into the flour mixture to combine. Use your hands to squeeze the moisture from the grated apple and carrots then add to the mixture, along with the walnuts and stir just to combine.

Transfer the mixture to the prepared loaf pan and level the top. Bake in the preheated oven for about 1–1¼ hours, until a skewer inserted in the centre of the cake comes out clean.

Leave the cake to cool in the pan for a few minutes then turn out onto a wire rack to cool. Slice as you would bread to serve. The cake will keep in an airtight container for 4–5 days.

stollen

This is a delicious traditional Christmas sweet filled with rum-soaked fruits and plenty of marzipan.

finely grated zest of
1 unwaxed lemon

250 g/8 oz. marzipan

1 egg, beaten

100 g/7 tablespoons unsalted
butter, melted

150 g/1 cup icing/
confectioners' sugar

Rum-soaked fruits

250 g/1½ cups sultanas/
golden raisins

170 g/1½ cups mixed peel

80 ml/⅓ cup dark or golden
rum

Stollen dough

1 tablespoon dried quick yeast

70 g/⅓ cup golden caster/
granulated sugar

140 ml/½ cup plus
1 tablespoon whole milk,
warmed

1 large egg yolk

175 g/1½ sticks unsalted
butter, at room temperature

500 g/3¾ cups strong/bread
flour

*a baking sheet, lined with
parchment paper*

Makes 2 stollen

Prepare the rum-soaked fruits at least 24 hours in advance. Put the sultanas/golden raisins, mixed peel and rum in a bowl. Mix, cover and leave to rest for at least 24 hours.

When you are ready to make the stollen dough, stir the yeast and sugar into the warm milk and set aside for 5 minutes.

Put the yolk, butter and flour in a mixing bowl and add the yeast mixture. Mix until you get a smooth dough, then transfer to a lightly floured surface and knead for 5 minutes. The dough should be soft but not sticky. If it is sticky, add a little flour and knead again. Return the dough to the mixing bowl, dust in flour, cover and let rise for 1 hour in a warm place. The dough should increase significantly in size.

Stir the lemon zest into the rum-soaked fruits, then uncover your mixing bowl and pour in the soaked fruits. Knead the dough again to incorporate and evenly distribute the fruits. Divide the dough in two, cover, and let rise for another 40 minutes in a warm place.

Roll one ball of dough out with a rolling pin into a rough square about 5 mm/¼ inch thick. Take half the marzipan and roll it into a tube slightly shorter than the square of dough. Place it along one side of the dough and start to roll the dough up from that side. Keep the sides tucked in as you roll. Repeat with the other ball of dough and remaining marzipan. Brush the beaten egg over the stollen. Cover and let rise for another 30 minutes in a warm place.

Preheat the oven to 200°C (400°F) Gas 6.

Put the logs on the prepared baking sheet and bake in the preheated oven for 10 minutes, then reduce the heat to 190°C (375°F) Gas 5 and bake for another 20 minutes. Remove from the oven and brush the stollen generously with melted butter. Dust with icing/confectioners' sugar and leave to cool.

Christmas bread with orange, fennel and raisins

This pretty loaf of bread is slightly sweet and the ideal partner to a cheeseboard; it marries particularly well with milder cheeses, such as Jarlsberg and young Brie.

500 ml/2¼ cups buttermilk

14 g/4½ teaspoons (2 envelopes) easy-blend dried yeast

3 tablespoons golden syrup, maple syrup or honey

grated zest of 1 unwaxed orange

1 teaspoon fennel seeds, freshly ground

½ tablespoon sea salt

200 g/1½ cups wholemeal rye/unbleached bread flour

500 g/3⅓ cups strong white/unbleached bread flour

40 g/¼ cup raisins

To finish

1 egg, lightly beaten

a handful of blanched almonds

2 baking sheets, lined with parchment paper

Makes 2 loaves

Heat the buttermilk in a small saucepan until lukewarm. Whisk in the yeast and syrup or honey, remove from the heat and let stand for 5 minutes.

Transfer the buttermilk mixture to a large mixing bowl and stir in the orange zest, ground fennel and salt. Start adding the flours, first by whisking and then, when the mixture gets too stiff, with a wooden spoon. When all the flour has been added, you should have a firm dough. Cover with a clean dish towel and let rise in a warm place for 30 minutes.

After 30 minutes, knead the raisins into the dough. Divide the dough into two and shape into round loaves. Place each loaf on a prepared baking sheet. Cover with the dish towel again and let rest in a warm place for 30 minutes.

Preheat the oven to 200°C (400°F) Gas 6.

Brush the surface of the loaves with the beaten egg and press the almonds gently into the dough to make a pretty pattern. Bake in the preheated oven for 40 minutes, but if the bread looks well browned after about 30 minutes, lower the temperature to 150°C (300°F) Gas 2 for the last few minutes.

a cup of
cheer

bloody mary with celery salt

Bloody Mary, a classic brunch drink, just gets better with a rim of celery salt. When making the celery salt, the leaves are dried in the oven on a wire rack so that warm air can circulate around the leaves.

1 small bunch celery, with leaves
1 tablespoon Jurassic salt
ice
1.25 litres/5 cups chilled tomato or vegetable juice
250 ml/1 cup chilled citron vodka
3 teaspoons Worcestershire sauce
2 teaspoons hot sauce or Tabasco sauce
1 tablespoon balsamic vinegar
finely grated zest and freshly squeezed juice of 1 lemon (reserve the squeezed fruits)
cracked green peppercorns

Serves 4

Preheat the oven to its lowest setting. Pick the leaves from the celery, place on a wire rack and put in the oven for 10–15 minutes until they are dried. Remove from the oven and let cool.

When ready to serve, put the dried celery leaves and Jurassic salt in a mini food processor or a salt grinder, grind and empty onto a small plate. Wet the rims of 4 glasses with the reserved lemon shells and dip them in the celery salt.

Fill a tall jug/pitcher with ice and pour in the tomato juice, vodka, Worcestershire sauce, hot sauce, balsamic vinegar and lemon zest and juice. Season liberally with cracked green peppercorns and a little of the celery salt. Stir and pour into the salt-rimmed glasses. Garnish each with a celery stick and serve.

black olive martini

3 cured black olives, pitted
1 sprig fresh rosemary
1 teaspoon dry vermouth, such as Noilly Prat
60 ml/2½ oz. gin
ice

Serves 1

Skewer the olives on the rosemary sprig. Pour the vermouth into a chilled glass, swirl and pour out. Fill a cocktail shaker with ice and pour in the gin. Shake and strain the gin into the glass.

Garnish with the olive skewer and serve immediately.

garrick gin punch

50 ml/2 oz. London dry gin
25 ml /1 oz. fresh lemon juice
12.5 ml/½ oz. maraschino liqueur
a dash of sugar syrup
2 dashes Angostura bitters
lemon zest, to garnish

Serves 1

Add all the ingredients to a cocktail shaker filled with ice and shake together until the outside of the shaker starts to frost.

Strain into a frosted coupette glass and serve garnished with a thin piece of lemon zest.

the hot toddy

50 ml/2 oz. Scotch whisky
20 ml/scant 1 oz. clear honey
25 ml/1 oz. fresh lemon juice
a pinch of ground cinnamon or 1 cinnamon stick
boiling water, to top up
2 pieces of lemon zest, studded with cloves, to garnish

Serves 1

Add all the ingredients to a heatproof glass and stir gently to mix. Top up with boiling water and serve garnished with a piece of lemon zest studded with cloves.

negus

There always seems to be plenty of port around during the festive season, and rightly so, but if you're looking for something more complex for your port, look no further than the Negus.

75 ml/3 oz. Tawny port
25 ml/1 oz. fresh lemon juice
10 ml/2 barspoons sugar syrup
boiling water, to top up
lemon zest, to garnish
grated nutmeg, to serve

Serves 1

Add the port, sugar and lemon juice to a heatproof glass and stir gently to mix. Top up with boiling water and serve garnished with a piece of lemon zest and dusted with nutmeg.

harvest punch

1 litre/4 cups (hard) cider
300 g/1½ cups brown sugar
1 teaspoon allspice
1 teaspoon ground nutmeg
1 teaspoon ground cinnamon
apple slices studded with cloves, to garnish

Serves 6

Add all the ingredients to a saucepan set over medium heat and simmer gently for 1 hour, stirring frequently.

Remove from the heat and pour into a heat-resistant punch bowl. Serve in heat-resistant punch cups or glasses, garnished with apple slices studded with cloves.

mulled wine

Traditionally made with red wine, sugar and spices, this drink is always served hot. Try not to let your mixture boil when you heat it as this may impair the flavor.

2 x 750-ml/25 fl. oz. bottles red wine

100 ml/⅓ cup brandy

pared zest and freshly squeezed juice of 2 clementines

pared zest of one lime

pared zest of one lemon

200 g/1 cup caster/ superfine sugar

1 cinnamon stick

4 cloves

4 pinches of grated nutmeg

1 split vanilla bean

lemon zest and cinnamon sticks, to garnish

Serves 10

Add all the ingredients to a large saucepan set over medium heat. Simmer gently for about 30 minutes, stirring occasionally.

Serve in heatproof glasses garnished with extra lemon zest and cinnamon sticks.

hot buttered rum

3 teaspoons light brown soft sugar

50 ml/2 oz. dark rum

½ teaspoon allspice

1 teaspoon butter

hot water, to top up

a piece of orange zest studded with cloves, to garnish

Serves 1

Warm a heatproof glass and add the sugar and a little hot water. Stir until the sugar has dissolved and then add the rum, allspice and butter. Top up with hot water and stir until the butter has melted.

Garnish with a piece of orange zest studded with cloves, and serve.

Catalan coffee punch

This is a traditional hot coffee and rum drink from the Catalonia region of Spain. The alcohol is burnt off before the coffee is added. It is traditional to use a terracotta cooking vessel for this, but a stainless-steel saucepan will work just as well. Be careful when igniting the rum. Use an extra-long match or a taper to keep your hands well away from the flame.

250 ml/1 cup white rum
1–2 tablespoons caster/superfine sugar
1 cinnamon stick
2 strips unwaxed lemon zest
500 ml/2 cups freshly brewed hot coffee

Serves 6–8

Put the rum, sugar, cinnamon and lemon zest in a flameproof dish and carefully ignite the mixture. Let the flame die down completely, then slowly pour in the hot coffee. Divide between heavy-based shot glasses or heatproof demitasse cups and serve.

Portuguese mulled port

Similar to mulled wine but made using port, this is an elegant spiced punch perfect for a winter cocktail party. It is fairly potent so serve it in small demitasse cups (or glasses) as an aperitif.

2 unwaxed oranges
500 ml/2 cups water
50 g/¼ cup light brown soft sugar
10 cloves, lightly crushed
6 allspice berries, crushed
1 cinnamon stick, crushed
¼ teaspoon freshly grated nutmeg
1 bottle ruby port, 75 cl

Serves 12

Peel and slice 1 orange and squeeze the juice from the second orange. Put the slices and juice in a saucepan and add the water, sugar, cloves, allspice, cinnamon stick and nutmeg. Bring slowly to the boil, stirring until the sugar is dissolved.

Simmer gently for 10 minutes. Stir in the port and heat gently, without boiling, for a further 2–3 minutes. Strain and pour into small cups or heatproof glasses to serve.

peppermint white chocolate dream

A soothing after-dinner drink is a perfect way to end your day. You can just as easily use dark/bittersweet chocolate here if you prefer.

500 ml/2 cups milk
100 g/3½ oz. white chocolate, chopped
½ teaspoon peppermint extract
125 ml/½ cup double/heavy cream
grated white chocolate, to serve

Serves 2

Put the milk, chocolate and peppermint extract in a saucepan and heat gently until the chocolate is melted. Use a milk frother or balloon whisk to beat the mixture until it is light and foamy.

Divide between 2 heatproof glasses, whip the cream until thick and spoon on top of the drinks. Sprinkle with a little grated white chocolate and serve immediately.

mochaccino

Strong espresso coffee is combined here with chocolate to make a delicious and rich-tasting mocha drink.

50 g/2 oz. dark/bittersweet chocolate, grated
2 shots freshly brewed hot espresso coffee
250 ml/1 cup milk
125 ml/½ cup whipping cream, whipped
chocolate-coated coffee beans and grated
dark/bittersweet chocolate, to serve

Serves 2

Put the chocolate in 2 small cups and pour a shot of hot espresso into each one. Stir well until the chocolate is melted. Meanwhile, heat the milk in a small saucepan until hot, then use a milk frother or balloon whisk to froth the milk. Pour it over the coffee and top with whipped cream, chocolate-coated coffee beans and a sprinkle of grated chocolate. Serve immediately.

white Christmas

This is a delicious Christmas drink bursting with the evocative flavors of the festive season, such as orange zest and warm spices. For a large crowd, simply double or triple the ingredients as required. If you like frothy drinks (such as cappuccino), then a milk frother is an absolute must in your kitchen. There are various types available but basically they are devices that froth milk into foam until it is 'stiff' enough to be spooned on top.

1 litre/4 cups milk

200 g/7 oz. white chocolate, grated

2 unwaxed orange slices

4 cloves, lightly crushed

2 cinnamon sticks, lightly crushed

a pinch of freshly grated nutmeg

75 ml/⅓ cup Grand Marnier, Cointreau or other orange-flavored liqueur

125 ml/½ cup double/heavy cream, whipped

candied orange and grated white chocolate, to serve

Serves 6

Put the milk, chocolate, orange and spices in a saucepan and heat gently, stirring, until it just reaches boiling point. Froth the milk with a milk frother or whisk vigorously with a flat or small round whisk until the mixture is foamy.

Divide between 6 small cups or heatproof glasses and pour in the Grand Marnier. Spoon a little whipped cream on top of each drink and sprinkle with candied orange and grated white chocolate to serve.

spiced coconut milk

250 ml/1 cup milk
250 ml/1 cup coconut milk
1½ tablespoons light brown soft sugar
2 star anise, lightly crushed
1 small red chilli/chile, halved lengthwise and deseeded
125 ml/½ cup double/heavy cream
toasted shredded coconut, to serve

Serves 2

Put all the ingredients, except the cream, in a saucepan. Heat gently for 10 minutes then bring just to boiling point. Strain into 2 cups.

Whip the cream until it holds its shape and spoon over the drinks. Sprinkle with a little toasted coconut to serve.

marshmallow chocolate melt

500 ml/2 cups milk
½ teaspoon vanilla extract
6 large marshmallows
30 g/1 oz. dark/bittersweet chocolate
(at least 70% cocoa solids), broken into pieces

Serves 2

Put the milk and vanilla extract in a saucepan and heat gently until it comes to the boil. Remove from the heat. Pour the milk into 2 cups and top with the marshmallows.

Meanwhile, melt the chocolate in a small heatproof bowl set over a pan of gently simmering water (don't let the bowl touch the water or the chocolate will be spoiled). Drizzle the melted chocolate over the top of the drinks and serve immediately.

polar bear

Kahlúa is a coffee-flavored liqueur, which when combined with chocolate and cream looks innocent enough in a glass, but don't be deceived by looks – this deliciously creamy cocktail packs a punch! It's very rich and filling so it could easily be served as an alternative to dessert.

250 ml/1 cup milk
250 ml/1 cup double/heavy cream
75 g white chocolate, grated
80 ml/⅓ cup Kahlúa or other coffee-flavored liqueur
125 ml/½ cup double/heavy cream, whipped
grated white chocolate and white-chocolate-coated coffee beans, to serve

Serves 2

Put the milk and cream in a saucepan and heat gently until it just reaches boiling point. Remove the pan from the heat and stir in the chocolate until melted, then add the Kahlúa. Divide between 2 heatproof glasses or cups.

Whip the cream until thick, then spoon it over the drinks. Sprinkle with grated white chocolate and top with a few white-chocolate-coated coffee beans to serve.

hot chocolate cups with whipped almond cream

This is a rich, decadent chocolate drink topped with whipped, almond-flavoured cream. Almond syrup is widely available in most supermarkets or specialty food stores, alternatively you could use a few drops of almond extract.

250 ml/1 cup milk
250 ml/1 cup single/light cream
100 g/3½ oz. dark/bittersweet chocolate
(at least 70% cocoa solids), grated
grated chocolate and flaked almonds, to serve

Whipped almond cream
125 ml/½ cup double/heavy cream
1 teaspoon almond syrup

Serves 4

Put the milk and cream in a saucepan and heat until almost boiling. Add the chocolate and stir over low heat until the chocolate is completely melted. Remove from the heat and let sit for 5 minutes.

To make the almond cream, whip the cream and almond syrup together until thickened. Pour the chocolate milk into 4 small cups, spoon the almond cream on top and serve sprinkled with grated chocolate and flaked almonds.

Turkish delight frothy

You can use any flavor Turkish delight you like in this pretty, delicate drink. The best bit is finding half-melted pieces of the Turkish delight at the bottom of the cup! Serve with a spoon.

500 ml/2 cups milk
50 g/2 oz. Turkish delight, cut into cubes, plus extra to top
125 ml/½ cup double/heavy cream, whipped
2 teaspoons rosewater
½ teaspoon clear honey
a pinch of ground cardamom
unsalted pistachio nuts, finely chopped, to serve

Serves 2

Put the milk and Turkish delight in a saucepan and heat gently, stirring constantly, until the mixture just reaches boiling point. Meanwhile, whip the cream, rosewater, honey and ground cardamom in a bowl until just stiff. Pour the milk into 2 cups and top with the cream. Sprinkle with pieces of Turkish delight and pistachio nuts and serve immediately.

peanut butter crunch

A big hit with the kids, this is a deliciously creamy, nutty drink.

500 ml/2 cups milk
3 tablespoons crunchy peanut butter
1 tablespoon maple syrup
60 ml/¼ cup double/heavy cream, whipped
ground cinnamon, to serve

Serves 2

Put the milk, peanut butter and maple syrup in a saucepan and heat gently, stirring constantly, until it just reaches boiling point and the peanut butter has melted. Froth the mixture using a balloon whisk.

Divide between 2 heatproof glasses or cups. Whip the cream until it holds its shape and spoon over the drinks. Dust with a little cinnamon to serve.

sleep tight milk

Lavender soothes the body and mind which makes it the perfect ingredient for a bedtime drink. You can use either fresh or dried lavender flowers, but remember if you use dried they are three times as strong, so use sparingly. If using fresh flowers or stems, make sure the lavender is free from pesticides. If you grow your own lavender, use that; dried lavender is available from specialty food stores.

500 ml/2 cups milk
1 tablespoon lavender flowers
2 teaspoons honey, preferably lavender
freshly grated nutmeg, to serve

Serves 2

Put the milk, lavender and honey in a saucepan and heat gently until the milk just reaches boiling point. Remove from the heat and let infuse for 10 minutes.

Strain the milk into 2 cups and serve dusted with a little freshly grated nutmeg.

rosemary milk

Rosemary may seem an unusual addition to a milky drink but not only is the flavour wonderful, rosemary has many health benefits too. It has long been known to soothe upset stomachs, aid digestion and help prevent headaches. This drink has an interesting, aromatic flavour.

500 ml/2 cups milk
2 large fresh rosemary sprigs, crushed
1–2 teaspoons light brown soft sugar, to taste

Serves 2

Put the milk and rosemary sprigs in a saucepan and heat very gently until it just reaches boiling point. Remove from the heat and let infuse for 5 minutes. Strain the milk into 2 cups, add sugar to taste and serve.

There really is nothing better than coming home on a cold winter's day, kicking off your boots and relaxing by the fire with a mug of hot cocoa.

recipe credits

Fiona Beckett
Parmesan Custards with Anchovy Toasts
Cheddar and Cider Fondue
Cheese and Basil Soufflés
Cheesy Toasts
Tartiflette
Saffron Risotto with Aged Parmesan, Sage and Serrano Ham
Extra-Crispy Macaroni Cheese
Cheese, Apple and Hazelnut Autumn Salad
Blue Cheese and Steak Winter Salad

Annie Rigg
Sole Goujons
Chicken Liver Parfait with Fig Relish and Toasted Brioche
Baked Goat Cheese with Herbed Ciabatta Croutons and Winter Fruit Salad
Very Herby Falafel with Red Pepper Hummus
Carrot and Chickpea Pancakes with Hummus and Slow-Roasted Tomatoes
Spiced Fried Chicken
Sticky Spare Ribs with Honey and Soy Glaze
Creamy Pancetta and Onion Tart
Meat Balls with Spiced Tomato Sauce
Spicy Potatoes

Misa Miink
Egg-Rice Pockets
Meat Pie
Arctic Roll with Vanilla and Chocolate
Orange and Poppy Seed Cake
Ginger Cake
Christmas Bread with Orange, Fennel and Raisins

Ben Reed
Garrick Gin Punch
Harvest Punch
Mulled Wine
The Hot Toddy
Negus
Hot Buttered Rum

Lydia France
Warm Spice-Rubbed Potatoes with Rosemary Mayonnaise

Isidora Popovic
Leek and Cheddar Mini Quiches
White Chocolate and Coffee Truffle Brownies
Rhubarb Custard and Crumble Tartlets
Pecan and Bourbon Tartlets
Chocolate and Chestnut Tart
Pumpkin and Cinnamon Strudel
Cranberry, Sherry and Vine Fruit Cake
Stollen

Fiona Smith
Spicy Bean Dip
Poppy Seed and Garlic Bagel Toasts
Iceberg, Blue Cheese and Date Salad
Roasted Sweet Potato and Macadamia Nut Salad
Pork and Lentil Salad
Bacon, Egg and Bean Salad with Grilled Chorizo on Toast
Roast Duck, Sausage, Sweet Potato and Cherry Salad

Valerie Aikman-Smith
Spicy Pork Satay with Roast Salted Peanut Sauce
Olive Suppli
Popcorn with Spiced Salt
Golden Potato Crisps with Truffle Salt
Mustard and Herb Chicken Baked in a Salt Crust
Jasmine-Brined Roasted Poussins with Salsa Verde

Chocolate Sea Salt Cookies
Bloody Mary with Celery Salt
Black Olive Martini

Ross Dobson
Salt Cod, Potato and Butter Bean Fritters
Barley Risotto with Mushrooms and Goat Cheese
Seafood and Yellow Split Pea Curry
Slow-Cooked Pork Belly with Beans and Miso
Slow-Cooked Lamb Shanks with Lentils
Spanish Bread Salad with Chickpeas, Chorizo and Baby Spinach
Poached Chicken and Brown Rice Salad with Ginger and Lime
Slow-Cooked Lamb Salad with Beans, Pomegranate and Fresh Mint
Hot Smoked Salmon and Cannellini Bean Salad with Gremolata
Pastry Cigars with Halloumi
Oaty Apple and Raisin Crumble
Vanilla Rice Pudding

Tonia George
French Onion Soup
Minestrone with Parmesan Rind
Cauliflower and Stilton Soup
Pea and Smoked Ham Soup with Mint
Split Pea and Sausage Soup
Corn and Pancetta Chowder
Beef, Tamarind and Sweet Potato Soup
Vietnamese Beef Pho
Seafood Tom Yam
Simple Relishes
Flavoured Butters
Croutons etc.
Taleggio and Sage Focaccia Rolls
Red Pepper Scones
Cornbread Muffins

Laura Washburn
Vegetable Gratin with Fresh Herbs and Goat Cheese
Ham and Blue Cheese Gratin

Salmon, Brocoli and Potato Gratin with Pesto
Mashed Potato Pie with Bacon, Leeks and Cheese
Smoked Trout Hash with Horseradish Cream
Tuna Noodle Casserole
Artichoke, Mushroom and Olive Pasta Bake with Provolone
Sausage, Pasta and Bean Stew with Greens
Chicken Pot Pie with Tarragon and Leeks
Steak, Leek and Mushroom Pie with Guiness
Moroccan Chicken Pie
Smoked Haddock and Potato Gratin
Tamale Pie
Fish Pie with Leeks and Herbs
Braised Pot Roast with Red Wine, Rosemary and Bay Leaves
Spicy Pork Stew with Sweet Potatoes and Beans
Farmhouse Chicken Casserole with Carrots, Leeks and Potato
Asian Beef Braise with Pak-Choi
Ginger and Star Anise Braised Chicken
Hungarian Goulash
Spiced Lamb Tagine with Prunes
Moroccan Fish Tagine
Thai Red Beef Curry
Coconut Chicken Curry with Lentil Dhal and Potatoes
Sweet Potato, Spinach and Chickpea Stew with Coconut
Root Vegetable Gratin
Butternut Squash, Corn and Bread Bake with Cheese and Chives
Winter Vegetable Bake
Apple, Beetroot and Fennel Salad with Roquefort
Roasted Butternut Squash with Spiced Lentils, Goat Cheese and Walnuts
Tart Tatin
Pear and Almond Tart
Dutch Apple Pie
Classic Apple Pie
Pear Cobbler
Pear Clafoutis with Figs and

Almonds
Apple and Blackberry Crumble
Spiced Pear Trifle
Baked Apples and Pears with Dried Fruit, Honey and Hazelnuts
Poached Pears
Apple and Carrot Bread with Walnuts

Sonia Stevenson
Roast Duck a l'alsacienne with Sauerkraut and Frankfurters
Spiced Roast Ham or Pork with Juniper Berries
Slow-Roasted Pork Loin with Rosemary, Madeira and Orange
Rolled Roast Pork with Sage and Onion Stuffing

Sarah Randall
Cherry Marzipan Streusel Squares
Hazelnut Cheesecake Bars
No-bake Chocolate, Macadamia and Fig Slices
Chocolate Heaven Muffins
Mini Chocolate and Cherry Cakes
Pear, Mascarpone and Orange Tarts
Brown Sugar Pavolva with Cinnamon Cream and Pomegranate
Chocolate Chestnut Brownie Torte
Tropical Chai Pineapple Cake
Blackcurrant, Berry and Hazelnut Crumble Cake
Mulled Wine and Cranberry Tea Bread

Louise Pickford
Catalan Coffee Punch
Portuguese Mulled Port
Mochaccino
Peppermint White Chocolate Dream
White Christmas
Spiced Coconut Milk
Marshmallow Chocolate Melt
Polar Bear
Hot Chocolate Cups with Whipped Almond Cream
Turkish Delight Frothy
Peanut Butter Crunch
Sleep Tight Milk
Rosemary Milk

photography credits

KEY: a = above, b = below, r = right, l = left, c = centre.

Jan Baldwin
pages 23 bl, 65

Steve Baxter
pages 16, 18, 20 b, 23 al, 25, 26 al & ar, 32, 102

Martin Brigdale
pages 6 ar & br, 54, 58, 62, 68, 71–72, 75–76, 79–80, 83, 84 al & br, 87–88, 96, 103, 110

Peter Cassidy
pages 4 c, 4 r, 8, 22, 23r, 24, 30–31, 41, 61, 69, 73, 89, 92 –93, 95, 108, 109 bl & ar, 112, 114, 117, 126 ar, 131, 135 bl & ar, 137–138, 141, 142 a, 143 bl,

144, 147–148, 151, 152 al & br, 156, 159, 161

Jonathan Gregson
pages 29 al & bl, 33, 99, 170

Andrea Jones
page 9

Richard Jung
pages 13, 17, 34 br, 52–53, 59, 67, 104, 106, 109 al, 118, 146, 152 ar, 158

Sandra Lane
page 163

William Lingwood
pages 26br, 160, 165–166, 167 ar &br, 168–169, 171, 172 al & bl, 173 al & bl

Mark Lohman
pages 38, 64, 101

Diana Miller
pages 50l, 113

Steve Painter
pages 10, 12, 14–15, 29r, 37, 46, 51, 77, 85, 91, 100, 111, 121, 132–134, 135al, 136, 139–140, 143r, 149, 153–154, 172r, 173r

William Reavell
pages 55, 78, 86, 94, 98, 145, 157

Claire Richardson
page 142 b

Yuki Sugiura
pages 34 al, 35r, 36, 40, 42–44, 47–49, 50 bl & br

Debi Treloar
pages 11, 39, 107, 143 al,

Chris Tubbs
page 1

Jo Tyler
pages 128, 162

Kate Whitaker
pages 6 al & bl, 7, 19, 27–28, 35l, 45, 56, 60, 70, 74, 82, 97, 115–116, 119–120, 123, 124–125, 126 al & br, 127, 129–130, 150, 152bl, 155, 164, 167l

Isobel Wield
page 66

Polly Wreford
pages 63, 105

Edina van der Wyck
pages 3, 4

endpapers front and back © David Tomlinson / Lonely Planet Images
page 2 © Myles New/Country Homes and Interiors/IPC+ Syndication
page 5 © Simon Whitmore/Woman & Home/IPC+ Syndication
page 21 © Ideal Home/IPC+ Syndication
page 57 © Woman and Home/ Oliver Gordon / /IPC+ Syndication
page 81 © Buero Monaco/Corbis
page 84ar © Brent Darby/Country Homes and Interiors/IPC+Syndication
page 84bl © Tim Winter / Ideal Home/IPC+ Syndication
page 90 © Ideal Home/IPC+ Syndication
page 122 © Dave J Hogan/ Getty Images